FIFTEEN

SECRETS

for
Life
and
Ministry

Robert R. Kopp

Fifteen Secrets for Life and Ministry by
Robert R. Kopp
ISBN # 0-89228-151-0

Copyright © 2004
by Robert R. Kopp

Published by
Impact Christian Books, Inc.
332 Leffingwell Ave.,
Kirkwood, MO 63122
314-822-3309
www.impactchristianbooks.com

Cover Design: *Ideations*

**Dedicated
to**

The Rev. Harold F. Mante who enfleshed *agape,*

**Osceola, Logans Ferry, and Bethany for the privilege of
partnership,**

**friends who cannot be named lest acquaintances be
offended,**

family, and, of course,

Our Lord and Savior Jesus!

Colossians 3:1-2

Fifteen Secrets for Life and Ministry

Contents

Preface ....*vii*

Secret 1 11
Secret 2 21
Secret 3 39
Secret 4 53
Secret 5 65
Secret 6 79
Secret 7 103
Secret 8 113
Secret 9 133
Secret 10 147
Secret 11 159
Secret 12 171
Secret 13 187
Secret 14 201
Secret 15 223

Vita..234

Preface
to
Secrets for Life and Ministry

Bless the Lord, O my soul, and all that is within me,
Bless His holy name!
Psalm 103

Discerning God's will doesn't take any guesswork.

Who God is and what God expects from the faithful have been revealed clearly, concisely, and conclusively in Jesus according to the Bible.

The answers to faith and moral issues are exemplified in Jesus and explained in the Bible.

Though rare and exceptional, there are issues that seem to evade the profile of Jesus and prescriptions of the Bible.

For example, while teaching homiletics at Kansas City's Nazarene Theological Seminary in the early 80s, I often made this comment: "If the text is not clear to you after using your primary exegetical tools, read as many commentaries on it that you can find. If they all agree on the translation and interpretation, you can preach that truth without fear of affronting God's holiness. But if there is significant disagreement, stop, pray, and study some more; and don't stop praying and studying until your discoveries have been confirmed by others in consonance with Jesus and the Bible."

This is my way of saying the following secrets for life and ministry are consistent with God's apocalyptic will as exemplified in Jesus and explained in the Bible to the best of my discernment after over 30 years of ordained life and ministry.

Yet sorely aware of my carnalities, I may need correction on some of them. It's like Paul observed as counsel, "All have sinned and fall short of the glory of God" (Romans 3:23).

So if I'm wrong from what you've discerned from your relationship with Jesus as informed by the Bible, let me know.

If you'd like to add some secrets of your own, please do as long as you're convinced they are in consonance with Jesus and the Bible.

Knowing our Lord won't be finished with us until the roll is called up yonder, I'm not suggesting this list is exhaustive or final.

I'm just saying they've helped me to survive with the intention of becoming increasingly faithful.

That's why I'm sharing them with you.

I pray our Lord is honored, you are helped, and the Kingdom is advanced with or without my cooperation.

Fifteen Secrets for Life and Ministry

1. Remembering you're going to live a lot longer with Jesus than anybody else makes establishing life's priorities a no-brainer.

2. Don't blame Jesus for Christians (or churches).

3. People with actual authority over our lives are not acknowledged as authority over our lives unless they are in consonance with God's apocalyptic will exemplified in Jesus and explained in the Bible.

4. Trying to be rational with the irrational is illogical; the ancillary being, being wrong invalidates argument and being right does not necessitate it.

5. Knowing people get ticked off about almost anything anyway, tick 'em off on your terms; doing your best, intentionally and humbly, to bring your terms into consonance with God's apocalyptic will exemplified in Jesus and explained in the Bible.

6. Pejorative instincts (aka original sin) require perpetual confession and repentance for redemptive dispensations.

7. Borrowing a line, "It is better to light a candle than curse the darkness."

8. While never underestimating *poneros,* never doubt Jesus as *kurios* of all.

9. We are not responsible for the beliefs and behaviors of others; but we are responsible for our response.

10. Holiness = Happiness (i.e., the holier we are, the happier we are!).

11. When you think you've arrived, it's time to start over.

12. If you don't have calluses on your knees, they're on your mind, heart, and soul.

13. Energy and enthusiasm for Jesus confirm belief in Jesus; the corollary being, if you're not excited about Jesus, He doesn't show in your confession (what you say), conduct (what you do), or countenance (how you appear).

14. Corporate Christians (apostate, moderate, and evangelical) have just enough of Jesus to feel comfortable about themselves (i.e., spiritually anesthetized) but not enough to be any real good for God's sake; knowing true discipleship puts personal and vocational securities at risk.

15. Jesus is counting on you!

SECRET 1

Remembering you're going to live a lot longer with Jesus than anybody else makes establishing life's priorities a no-brainer.

I'll never forget shopping for a cross about 25 years ago in a big mall jewelry store near Edison, New Jersey.

When I asked the salesman if he'd let me see the store's stock of crosses, he asked, "Do you want one with or without the little man on it?"

For too many years, I laughed that off as just another gross example of our culture's spiritual ignorance.

But about four years ago while struggling with my personal Pauline angst to overcome carnalities with holiness to honor God's saving grace in my life through Jesus (see Romans 7:7-8:1), I began to ask myself, "How real is my faith? Is it with or without practical obedience to Jesus?"

I realized too much of my life had been a pathetic yes to the hymn's rhetorical question, "Must Jesus bear the cross alone and all the world go free?"

Like too many believers who think God's grace is license to ignore behavioral expectations for believers exemplified in Jesus and explained in the Bible, I wasn't serious about the hymn's prescriptive answer: "No, there's a cross for everyone, and there's a cross for me."

Unlike too many of today's clergy whose persecution for righteousness' sake barely exceeds complaints for hymn selections and liturgies resembling sacred laundry lists and personal sacrifice compromised by obsessive attention to

11

vouchers for anything from facial tissue supplies to mileage reimbursements, German Lutheran pastor and professor Dietrich Bonhoeffer understood the cost of discipleship.

Captured for conspiring to assassinate Hitler because he believed it was not only his responsibility to care for the victims of a mad motorist but also to do all in his power to remove the madman from the wheel, Bonhoeffer was executed at Flossenbürg's extermination camp on the direct order of Himmler on 9 April 1945.

Assured of eternal security because of Jesus, Bonhoeffer whispered with incontrovertible confidence to young English Captain Payne Best just steps from the gallows, "This is the end, for me the beginning of life."

Bonhoeffer's behavior confirmed his belief in Jesus who promised so clearly, concisely, and conclusively, "If anyone would come after me, let him deny himself and take up his cross and follow me. For whoever would save his life will lose it, but whoever loses his life for my sake will find it" (Matthew 16:24-25).

Less than a decade earlier, Bonhoeffer wrote about walking (behavior) the talk (belief) of Christianity (*The Cost of Discipleship*, 1937),

> The cross is laid on every Christian... When Christ calls a man, he bids him come and die. It may be a death like that of the first disciples who had to leave home and work to follow Him, or it may be a death like Luther's, who had to leave the monastery and go out into the world. But it is the same death every time—death in Jesus Christ, the death of the old man at his call...The wounds and scars he receives in the fray are living tokens of this participation in the cross of his Lord... Suffering, then, is the badge of true discipleship. The disciple is not above his master...That is the only path to victory. The cross is his triumph over suffering.

It's Secret 1 for life and ministry: "Remembering you're going to live a lot longer with Jesus than anybody else makes establishing life's priorities a no-brainer."

Practically, other rhetorical questions have emerged; providing daily accountability for my life and ministry:

- Do I live like Jesus is Lord of my life?
- Do I live like I know what I say and do express what I believe; and what I believe has eternal consequences?
- Do I live like Jesus is still dead and buried or risen and reigning as Almighty God with Father and Spirit?
- Could I prove my faith in a court of law?
- If love for Jesus were a crime, would I be convicted?
- If a gun were held to my head and I was told to deny Jesus or die, what would I do?
- And knowing there are opportunities to ally myself with Jesus or deny Him every day, how's my report card?

So I wear two crosses.

One is made of nails to remind me of what He did for me and what I must do for Him to prove faith's veracity.

The other was given to me at ordination. It's beautiful. It's the cross used as the seal for my old denomination (The United Presbyterian Church in the United States of America). A prominent Celtic cross is surrounded by porcelain inlays of other symbols highlighting God's sovereignty, Holy Spirit, Biblical revelation, and mission.

The porcelain has chipped over the years.

So have I.

John 3:17 comes to mind: "For God did not send His Son into the world to condemn the world, but in order that the world might be saved through Him."

That's why I feel compelled to take up His cross.

Salvation compels service.

Paul put it this way, "The only thing that counts is faith expressing itself through love" (Galatians 5:6).

It's a no-brainer.

It's how we *cross* rhetorical questions.

My generation has had a hard time adjusting to men wearing jewelry.

When I was growing up, men didn't wear necklaces except for military dog tags. Ringo was an aberration. And wearing earrings evoked the kind of gossip that really upset Middle American moms and dads.

But in addition to the crosses, I've got three rings!

My wedding band is a no-brainer. It reminds me and others of my covenant with my wife in the Lord.

The other two rings were crafted and purchased in a small jewelry shop just outside of the Jaffa Gate in Jerusalem, Israel. While both bands symbolize the Western Wall of the Temple to remind me of our roots in Judaism, one ring combines the Star of David with the cross while the other has an inlay of the Ten Commandments.

I guess I wear a lot of jewelry.

And as long as I don't show up in the pulpit with earrings, I can live with the generational paradox of not liking jewelry yet wearing so much of it.

My sense of call more than decision to wear such highly symbolic jewelry to inspire recollection of who God is and what God expects from me goes back to Deuteronomy 6:4-9:

> **Hear, O Israel: The Lord our God, the Lord is one. You shall love the Lord your God will all your heart and with all your soul and with all your might. And these words that I command you today shall be on your heart. You shall teach them diligently to your children, and shall talk of them when you sit in your**

house, and when you walk by the way, and when you lie down, and when you rise. You shall bind them as a sign on your hand, and they shall be as frontlets between your eyes. You shall write them on the doorposts of your house and on your gates.

Parenthetically, that's why you'll still see many Jews wearing phylacteries or small leather boxes containing verses of the Hebrew Scriptures on their foreheads and arms. That's why many Jewish homes have a mezuzah or box of Biblical verses attached to their doorposts.

The symbols direct attention to God.

They remind us of God's pre-eminent place in our lives– highlighting His character and the character of those praying and laboring to be faithful to Him.

They keep us focused in the spirit of Hebrews 12:2: "Let us fix our eyes on Jesus."

They encourage behavior in consonance with belief.

They provide an instrument of spiritual accountability.

Certainly, it's easy to assess life's priorities or who and what are really, really, really important to us.

It's easy to determine who and what attract most of our allegiance, attention, affirmation, and affection.

It's easy to calculate our commitments.

Just check out the seven Cs of life:

- Calendar (How do I spend my time?)
- Checkbook (How do I spend my money?)
- Church (How often am I there?)
- Confession (What I say!)
- Conduct (What I do!)
- Countenance (How I appear!)

15

• Chums (Do my friends and family draw me closer to or farther away from Jesus?)

Paul put it this way (2 Corinthians 6:14-18):

"Do not be unequally yoked with unbelievers. For what partnership has righteousness with lawlessness? Or what fellowship has light with darkness? What accord has Christ with Belial? Or what portion does a believer share with an unbeliever? What agreement has the temple with idols? For we are the temple of the living God; as God said, "I will make my dwelling among them and walk among them, and I will be their God, and they shall be my people. Therefore go out from their midst, and be separate from them, says the Lord, and touch no unclean thing; then I will welcome you, and I will be a father to you, and you shall be sons and daughters to me, says the Lord Almighty."

Simply, who and what we are yoked or tied to betrays our allegiance, attention, affirmation, and affection.

Are we yoked to pleasure, power, position, property, prejudices, persons, drugs, alcohol, gambling, eating, shopping, or other negative addictions?

Addiction to anyone or anything that draws us away from Jesus is a negative to damning yoke.

That's why He counseled, "Come to me, all who labor and are heavy laden, and I will give you rest. Take my yoke upon you, and learn from me, for I am gentle and lowly in heart, and you will find rest for your souls. For my yoke is easy, and my burden is light" (Matthew 11:28-30).

In other words, Jesus saves!

Yoking ourselves to Jesus enables confident living in the assurance of eternal life.

The key to overcoming the meanness, madness, and misery of life in the modern world is yoking or tying ourselves to Jesus in all things at all times in all places regardless of the company. That's why Augustine prayed (*The Confessions,* A.D. 397-400),

> You are great, O Lord, and greatly to be praised; great is your power and to your wisdom there is no limit...You have made us for yourself, and our heart is restless until it rests in you...Come into my heart and inebriate it, to the end that I may forget my evils and embrace you, my one good...Grant this, so that you may grow sweet to me above all the allurements that I followed after. May I love you most ardently, may I cling to your hand with all my heart...May whatever I speak and write, whatever I read and calculate, serve you.

When we're yoked to God as profiled in Jesus and prescribed in the Bible, we pray,

> Depending upon Your grace, O Lord, I will
> Go where You want me to go,
> Say what You want me to say, and
> Do what You want me to do.
> For the glory of Jesus in whose Name I pray.
> Amen!

You may have heard about the pastor waiting in line for gas just before a long holiday weekend. The attendant said to him, "I'm sorry about the delay, but it seems everyone waits until the last minute to get ready for a long trip." The pastor laughed, "I know what you mean. It's the same in my business."

But sooner or later, everybody reaches that apocalyptic moment when realizing the days spent are not nearly as many as the days left.

Someday everybody will return from the cemetery but you or me.

My hair stylist, Debbie Sue who is located about a block or two from the church, brought that to my attention not too long ago.

I like Debbie Sue.

She always laughs about bald guys like me carrying combs or trying to recapture youth through corrective combing.

Anyway, she said she knew I was a senior citizen because I have more hair growing out of my nose and ears than the top of my head.

I give a 30% tip to her for encouragement like that!

Nevertheless, advancing years have a way of enabling us to see the big picture.

Big parts of that picture came into focus for me when I read *If I Knew*:

> If I knew it would be the last time
> That I'd see you fall asleep,
> I would tuck you in more tightly
> and pray the Lord, your soul to keep.
>
> If I knew it would be the last time
> that I see you walk out the door,
> I would give you a hug and kiss
> and call you back for one more.
>
> If I knew it would be the last time
> I'd hear your voice lifted up in praise,
> I would video tape each action and word,
> so I could play them back day after day.

If I knew it would be the last time,
I could spare an extra minute
to stop and say "I love you,"
instead of assuming you would know I do.

If I knew it would be the last time
I would be there to share your day,
Well I'm sure you'll have so many more,
so I can let just this one slip away.

For surely there's always tomorrow
to make up for an oversight,
and we always get a second chance
to make everything just right.

There will always be another day
to say "I love you,"
And certainly there's another chance
to say our "Anything I can do?"

But just in case I might be wrong,
and today is all I get,
I'd like to say how much I love you
and I hope we never forget.

Tomorrow is not promised to anyone,
young or old alike,
And today may be the last chance
you get to hold your loved one tight.

So if you're waiting for tomorrow,
why not do it today?
For if tomorrow never comes,
you'll surely regret the day,

That you didn't take that extra time
for a smile, a hug, or a kiss
and you were too busy to grant someone,
what turned out to be their one last wish.

So hold your loved ones close today,
and whisper in their ear,
Tell them how much you love them
and that you'll always hold them dear.

Take time to say "I'm sorry,"
"Please forgive me," "Thank you," or "It's O.K."
And if tomorrow never comes,
you'll have no regrets about today.

If we really, really, really knew and believed that before now, our priorities would be in order already.

If your priorities are in order, you are a blessing to the Lord who has blessed you!

If your priorities are not in order, you've still got time to reshuffle your deck!

Just by the very fact that you're reading this means you've still got time to rededicate yourself to the Lord.

Jesus tells us how to put our priorities in order: "But seek first His Kingdom and His righteousness, and all these things will be given to you as well" (Matthew 6:33).

Or as I've come to understand: "Remembering you're going to live a lot longer with Jesus than anybody else makes establishing life's priorities a no-brainer."

SECRET 2

Don't blame Jesus for Christians (or churches).

I used to write out all of my prayers in good old Elizabethan English for Sunday worship services.

Five experiences changed that.

First, while some folks still think the King James language is the only tongue heard by our Lord, I kept messing up those Thees, Thous, Thys, haths, saiths, arts, untos, shalts, shouldsts, begats, begots, beggeths, beseecheths, and so on.

Second, I couldn't read my own handwriting; confirming advancing years and the rumor that I write in tongues.

Third, it's really hard to integrate a young child's prayer request card for a dying hamster or young brother who should be damned for breaking the Play Station 2 when your previously prepared prayer is focused on the implications of double predestination in a world of religious pluralism.

Fourth, as I was reading off one Sunday morning prayer written on Saturday evening, I thought I heard our Lord say, "Bob, we went over that last night. Do you have anything else to talk about today?"

Fifth, I remembered the woman who complained to a friend about his prayers. He responded, "Listen, lady, I wasn't talking to you anyway!"

I mention those revelations because women and men paid to be holy like me (aka clergy) are often asked to be official pray*ers* at everything from opening day at the rodeo or Little League to the dedication of public ornaments.

Yet in our politically correct (corrupt?) culture which likes to pretend everybody "kind of believes" the same things about someone somewhere out there without any specificity betraying real religious diversity, it's risky business to pray in public.

I remember being the official pray*er* on the first day of an art show in Clark, New Jersey's borough building about 23 years ago.

I was confronted by an angry man just after praying who yelled at me in front of everybody for my lack of sensitivity to cultural inclusion by ending my prayer "in the name of Jesus."

"Well, excuuuuuuuse me," I thought to myself.

Not wanting to incite a jihad, I tried to explain my religious heritage–not to mention my ordination as a Christian pastor–compelling me to pray in the name of Jesus because I belong to Jesus and I am beholden to Jesus by confession of Jesus as Lord and Savior.

I even quoted Colossians 3:17: "And whatever you do, in word or deed, do everything in the name of the Lord Jesus, giving thanks to God the Father through Him."

Then I added in a wasted attempt to evoke a conciliatory spirit, "You know, friend, just as you and I don't expect a Jew, Hindu, Buddhist, Muslim, or whatever to pray in the name of Jesus, I trust you don't want me to misrepresent myself by not praying according to my beliefs."

That didn't help.

The truth is Christians are expected by our culture to remain private about their faith in public.

Of course, that's really, really, really tough because a Christian's God said, "Let your light shine before others" (see Matthew 5:13-16).

How can a Christian shut up when Paul wrote, "If you confess with your mouth that Jesus is Lord and believe in your heart that God raised Him from the dead, you will be saved. For with the heart one believes and is justified, and with the mouth one confesses and is saved" (Romans 10:9-10)?

So ever since that art show in the Garden State, I've taken five minutes or more to talk about who I am within the context of what I believe whenever I speak in public; which seems to have relieved a lot of mutual stress when I'm with my friends at Rotary, Kiwanis, Junior League, and the like.

I'd rather confess my faith than force people to take a guess.

Besides, after fessing up about our differences, we can trust each other enough to pursue common goals.

It's like the meeting of rabbis and Christian clergy about manger scenes on public property in Cranford, New Jersey about a year after the art show. I said, "Let's be honest. We have an irreconcilable theological difference. We believe Jesus is God and you don't." An old rabbi stood and said, "My young Christian friend is right; and I'll be damned if he is right. But I am betting my soul that he is wrong just as much as he is betting his soul that he is right."

That cleared the air about our differences; enabling us to work on common concerns in relaxed trust.

While another's truth may generate discomfort, trust can never be established without admitting it.

What's the same cannot be discussed apart from what's different.

I'm a Christian.

That means I believe Jesus is Lord and Savior; providing the certain way to confident living and eternal life.

How I exercise my religion and how others exercise theirs is where we meet to explore the possibilities for positive pluralism and global amelioration.

But it won't happen if we keep telling each other to shut up.

Again, as a Christian, I am convinced Jesus is who He said He is: "I am the way, and the truth, and the life. No one comes to the Father except through me" (John 14:6).

As a Christian, I agree with Peter: "Salvation is found in no one else" (Acts 4:12).

While that confession may cause disdain from others, He is what Christianity is all about.

Not since reading Dietrich Bonhoeffer's *The Cost of Discipleship* (1937) has a book so overwhelmed me with the reality of costly Christocentric faith as Franklin Graham's *The Name* (2002).

I was especially convicted by these lines:

The Name of Jesus Christ is a lightning rod because Jesus Christ represents the division between good and evil, God and Satan, light and darkness, righteousness and sin, heaven and hell. The Name of Jesus shouts out a choice: "Whom will you serve, give your life to, depend upon?" Rebellious, self-willed, sinful people want to retain the right to decide for themselves which way they will take. Jesus denies this option. Speaking on His behalf, the Apostle Peter said, "For there is no other name under heaven given among men by which we must be saved."

Jesus is gentle, but He is not weak. He loves the sinner but is absolutely intolerant of sin. He is not a negotiator. He is Lord.

It is this bristling truth that invites intolerance toward Christians. Jesus did not say, "Do your own thing; all roads lead to God." That would have made Jesus "politically correct," but Jesus is not politically correct. He is Lord.

Then Dr. Graham introduced John 15:18-21: "His followers today must accept the eternal truth of what He said to His disciples." Jesus said,

If the world hates you, you know that it hated Me before it hated you. If you were of the world, the world would love its own. Yet because you are not of the world, but I chose you out of the world, therefore the world hates you. Remember the word that I said to you, "A servant is not greater than his master." If they persecuted Me, they will also persecute you. If they kept My word, they will keep yours also. But all these things they will do to you for My name's sake, because they do not know Him who sent Me.

Sadly, Jesus is not a problem for many cultural or corporate Christians and churches (see Secret 14).

I'm reminded of the pastor who said during a children's sermon, "When I say a word, I want you to tell me the first thing that pops into your mind." He said, "Frog." And a little boy yelled, "Jesus." Puzzled, the pastor asked, "Why did you say Jesus when I said frog?" The boy answered, "Because I know you didn't call us down here to talk about frogs."

Unfortunately, any connection between Jesus and too many Christians and churches is coincidental.

Aside from the perfunctory use of His name to punctuate the end of prayers, Jesus rarely comes up in ecclesiastical conversations.

I suspect the omission of His name from talk and walk exposes the lack of recognition of *or relationship with* Him.

Or as Cyndi Lauper sang, "I see your true colors."

Answer these questions honestly:

- Does the name of Jesus come up in your church with about as much frequency as frogs?
- Are you and your church known for praising and promoting Jesus?
- Do you, the officers, and members of your church talk about Jesus by name?
- If aliens arrived at your home or church and asked to be taken to your leader, to whom would you take them? President? Professor? Pastor? Presbytery? General Assembly? Diocese? Conference? Mayor? Council? Senator? Martha Stewart? Brett Favre? Would you mention Jesus first and foremost?

"Though people need Jesus more than anyone or anything," a friend observed, "too many churches come off like Barney is in the pulpit preaching to the Teletubbies."

It's nothing new.

In his treatise *To the Christian Nobility of the German Nation* (18 August 1520) which assailed apostasy in the church, Martin Luther concluded, "God may help His church through the laity, since the clergy, to whom this task more properly belongs, have grown quite indifferent."

It's nothing new.

When Jesus was arrested, even Peter who often trumpeted his loyalty denied Him to save his own skin. Identity with Jesus was not as important as temporal personal security when he responded to three queries about his kinship to Christ: "I do not know Him...I am not one of them...I do not know what you are talking about" (see Luke 22:54-62).

Jesus saw it coming: "The Son of Man must suffer many things and be rejected by the elders and chief priests and scribes, and be killed" (Luke 9:22).

It was predicted long ago by Isaiah: "He was despised and rejected by men; a man of sorrows, and acquainted with grief; and as one from whom men hide their faces, He was despised, and we esteemed Him not." The prophet even provided the nefarious impulse: "All we like sheep have gone astray; we have turned every one to his own way" (see Isaiah 53).

But you'd think that wouldn't be such a big problem after two thousand years of salvation history.

Some folks just never quite get Him.

We know Jesus is not Lord and Savior for those who cannot talk about Him and refuse to walk with Him.

We see their true colors.

For without exception, I have never seen a person who loved Jesus but did not want to walk with Him and talk about Him.

Talking about Jesus leads to walking with Jesus; and when walking with Jesus, it's impossible not to talk about Him.

Deeds come from creeds because creeds lead to deeds.

Behavior patterned after Jesus provides authenticity to beliefs about Jesus.

Undeniably, being a Christian can't always be assumed with church membership.

Putting it another way, walking into a church turns you into a Christian about as much as walking into McDonald's turns you into a Big N' Tasty; although your cost may be as cheap!

Invariably, everybody's got the kind of horror stories that prompted Gandhi to say he would have become a Christian if it were not for Christians.

Indeed, there are too many pretenders polluting church membership rolls – women and men with little to no faith who don't talk the talk or walk the walk. You know the kind. They repel more than compel people to embrace Jesus into their lives. They cause the once inquiring to say, "If that's what Jesus does for you, I don't want any part of Him."

I can also imagine Jesus looking at some of them and saying, "Please don't tell anybody that you know me. I don't want them to see what I haven't done for you."

There are folks in pastoral ministry and on membership rolls whose claims to Christianity make others want no part of it.

In no particular order, here's my list of "Christians" who give a bad name to Jesus:

- My romantic delusions about the church and church-goers were shattered during my first clergy meeting after ordination. A weary old pastor with about as much hair as I now have cried, "Just last night as I was going up the stairs to my bed, I asked Jesus to take my life right now because I've got to be more valuable to Him than the members of my church who

28

bitch about everything I say and do." It was my introduction to a basic axiom of ecclesiology: "If you'd like to know what it's like to be a pastor, put on a deerskin and go walking through the woods on the first day of hunting season."

- I voted for Jimmy Carter when he ran against President Ford. That was before learning he lived in Atlanta as a state senator at the same time as Martin Luther King, Jr. Senator Carter did not have the courage of his storied convictions to meet with Dr. King because it would have been political suicide in the late 60s.

  Carter's Christian behavior did not match his Christian beliefs; especially when it came to the unity demanded by Jesus that cuts through class, color, and culture barriers.

  In other words, Mr. Born Again Christian President Jimmy Carter sacrificed Christian principles for political expediency.

  That's why I'm not very impressed by his Nobel Peace Prize in 2002; recalling Yasser Arafat also picked up that check.

- I remember an associate pastor in Kansas City who got into big trouble with several church officers for protesting outside of an abortion mill. When criticized for his public display of disgust for America's increasingly wanton disrespect for the sanctity of all human life with the stern reminder that he was distressing the pro-abortion (*pro-choice* being a sad euphemism) people in the church as if a pastor's beliefs must be muted to appease the bigotries and apostasies of those who forget a Christian's Ultimate Employer, he said, "I guess you would have been offended by people who tried to stop the trains headed to Auschwitz."

  Too many pewsitters expect their pulpiteers to be good humor men agreeing with the last person that they've talked to instead of the salt that often stings before it heals.

  That pastor was forced out not too long after that; but the

officers who forced him out continue to rotate back onto their boards with lamentable regularity.

- I invited an African-American pastor to dinner at an exclusive country club in Winston-Salem, North Carolina. After he told me the club did not welcome anyone but WASPs, he asked how I could accept honorary membership in a club violating the socioeconomic inclusion for which Jesus sacrificed Himself on the cross.

  When I called the club's president to ask if that was true, he said no.

  But a few minutes later, I got a call from the recently retired Chairman of the Board of Wachovia Bank who warned more than informed, "Dr. Kopp, you have been awarded the privileges of our club like your predecessors; but you have not been invited to comment on our policies."

  The very next day, I was taken to lunch by my predecessor to another private club which was equally exclusive and asked in reference to a distinguished African-American pastor in our franchise, "Did that nigger _____ put you up to this?"

  The day after that, I met with a few "elders" who said I shouldn't be going to soul food kitchens with the African-American custodial staff. I said, "I know ya'll are used to owning people down here, but you're not going to tell me who I can and cannot hang out with on my nickel."

  I didn't last long after that exchange.

  That's why the hypocrisy of Democrats skewering Senator Trent Lott for racial insensitivity while keeping their hands and tongues off former card-carrying KKK member and continuing Senator Robert Byrd who uses the "N" word routinely doesn't surprise me. If parts of the church are still racially retarded, I don't expect too much from the rest of the world.

  If the church doesn't reflect the ethics of its Lord, it shouldn't expect those outside of the church to embrace Him.

  That's why it's hard to argue with those critics who want nothing to do with the church because it has so little to do with Jesus these days.

- A pastor in one of Pittsburgh's most prestigious and *fabulously-well-to-do* churches was booted because he didn't *fit in.*

It all started at a session meeting when an elder complained, "You need to know our pastor is visiting prisoners at the county jail. They're going to get out sooner or later. And when they get out, they'll want to come here because of our pastor."

Imagine that.

Some folks forget the Bible is bigger than their favorite parts. I guess some versions dropped Matthew 25.

- A wonderfully warm and spiritually articulate Jewish woman, who rivals the most benevolent people who ever crossed my path, asked me about Jesus, studied and prayed with me about Jesus, and then was baptized into Jesus.

Not long after that, she was told by a staff member that she couldn't teach Sunday School because she might infect children with her *Jewishness;* however, she was invited back to teach when the church was experiencing financial problems a few years later.

Everybody's got priorities!

And sometimes - *too many times in the church* - principles are sacrificed for less than *Godly* priorities.

My first reaction was to recall Archie Bunker who was scolded by Meathead, "You know, Archie, Jesus was a Jew." Archie responded, "No, he was not. He was a Christian."

Then I said, "There's only one person in this church who knows more about the New Testament than she does *and I'm not sure I do.*"

Then she received an anonymous letter.

I detest anonymous letters. They are born of the same mentality that anonymously promotes terror throughout the world. Make no mistake about it. People who drop bombs on buildings and people *anonymously* -cowards who do not have the courage to claim ownership for their beliefs and behaviors-are terrorists.

Here are some excerpts from that letter which I keep in my wallet to remind me that some demons do their worst work in the church:

This letter is not intended to be hurtful or taken as a personal attack... [Give me a break!]

The_____ Church is a Christian church. We don't need to be infiltrated with your Jewish ways. Jesus broke away from the Jews and we are a Christ-centered church. [Really? I doubt it if you represent pervasive attitudes!]

Bob Kopp is on a crusade to bring in all of the misfits and oddballs to _____ Church. All Bob cares about is getting numbers up for his own glory...

You will be happier...with your own kind...

Sincerely, A Concerned Christian
[Yeah, right!]

I guess some versions dropped John 17.

• Rosalie had been the church's administrative assistant for nearly 20 years. Though promised a pension not long after being hired, she was denied any benefits or privileges when she retired.

The *party* line was she was never promised benefits.

By that time, I trusted Rosalie a lot more than that church's mothers and fathers. As her brother Byron, a senior writer and columnist for the *Washington Observer-Reporter,* wrote about her while reflecting on her battles with cancer, "Unlike her four brothers, she seldom has said a bad word - either a curse word or something ugly, hurtful or gossipy to, or about anyone." That's true; though, on occasion, she would ask me if some members really ever heard or heeded the *love stuff* of Jesus as she mentioned those who contradicted her brother's assessment of her Christlike character.

So I investigated for myself.

32

I talked with a previous pastor, treasurer, and president of the trustees who she said had promised her on behalf of all.

The only one who denied the promise was the trustee who, quite frankly, was a terrible crank whose word held as much weight for me as Saddam Hussein's does on weapons of mass destruction.

Not long after Rosalie decided to press the issue, her retirement was foisted upon her because of cancer surgery which altered her speech. A few of the church's most prominent members said in a casual meeting, "We've got to encourage her to retire because she sounds like a retard and we don't want people calling the church to have bad first impressions."

Even McDonald's, which enthusiastically hires the mentally challenged, has higher ethics!

But I'll never forget the meeting in which she was fired for insisting the church reneged on the promise of benefits.

Unceremoniously and without warning as Rosalie tried to plead her case, she was told to hand in her keys and meet an elder at 9:00 a.m. the next morning who would "watch" as she cleaned out her desk and personals.

After almost two decades of faithfulness and confidentiality with the dirty linen of a notoriously "clubby" congregation, she was treated like dirt.

She left without pension, purse, or party.

And then like so many staff members before and after her, she was slandered mercilessly.

It was almost as bad as when they fired a youth director simply because he was overweight and didn't project an image to their liking.

While I find few things in life more pathetic than people who try to absolve themselves by pointing out the faults of others, it was the coldest and cruelest church in my entire experience as a pastor.

Redemption is not in their spiritual vocabulary.

That's just the short list.

There are more from where they came from!

And I'm sure you've got your list too.

It doesn't take too long for anyone who hangs around the church to discover Jesus isn't *regarded* as Lord by all.

As I look at the church, I often agree with Bob Dylan who sang as a caution, "But the enemy I see wears a cloak of decency."

That is the troubador's paraphrase of Matthew 7:15: "They come to you in sheep's clothing."

I've got a lot more horror stories to tell.

Those were just the ones that have really, really, really stayed with me over the years.

But I've got to tell you about the worst of all for me. My reflection in the mirror.

For whenever I see the sins of others and start getting a bit too judgmental, the Lord whispers into my ear: "What's that I see in your eye?" (see Matthew 7:1-6).

I'll say more about that in Secrets 6 and 11.

But, for now, let's just admit there's a lot of hypocrisy in the church.

Again, it's nothing new.

Jesus rebuked the religious pretenders of his day who talked but didn't walk their faith (see Matthew 23):

Woe to you, scribes and Pharisees, hypocrites! For you travel across sea and land to make a single proselyte, and when he becomes a proselyte, you make him twice as much a child of hell as yourselves.

The word is υποκριτης (*hypokrites*); which refers to people who *mask over* or conceal their true identity. It's pretending to be someone other than who you really are.

It's acting.

And even the most generous look at today's church and her "Christians" leads to the conclusion that there's a lot of acting going on in the realm of the holy.

Some folks are faking faith.

Any connection between them and Jesus is coincidental.

It's like the artist in Woody Allen's *Hannah and Her Sisters* said to his paramour after watching televangelism, "If Jesus were to come back and see what's being done in His name, He'd never stop throwing up" (cf. Revelation 3:14-22).

That's why Jerry Kirk, President of the National Coalition for the Protection of Children and Families, lamented during an address to confessing churches on 2 May 2001 in McMurray, Pennsylvania, "My biggest struggle is not with people who don't believe in God. My biggest problem is with people who say they believe in God but don't act like they believe in God."

Mark Twain was right: "The church is always trying to get other people to reform; it might not be a bad idea to reform itself a little by way of example."

Summarily, Christians often contradict the character of Christianity as exemplified in Jesus and explained in the Bible.

And there's always someone outside of the church relentlessly eager to tell those of us inside of the church about it *as if we don't know it.*

I think of the snotty little ivy leaguer who yelled at his university's chaplain, "The church is full of hypocrites." In what must have been an instant inspiration from the Holy Spirit, the chaplain yelled back, "You're right! And there's room for one more!"

Fortunately, aberrations to the truth do not change the truth.

False witnesses to Jesus do not change the truth about and from Jesus.

People who say *or pretend* they love Jesus but don't love like Jesus don't change the pure and perfect love of Jesus.

Secret 2 is an honest assessment of the terrible plague in today's church: "Don't blame Jesus for Christians (or churches)."

Jesus is Lord and Savior and anyone can experience confident living in the assurance of eternal life through faith in Him alone.

Though we'll get to it a little later in more detail, Secrets 7 and 9 must be standard operating procedures for the church: "It is better to light a candle than curse the darkness...We are not responsible for the beliefs and behaviors of others; but we are responsible for our response."

People who are praying and laboring to be faithful to Jesus cannot be paralyzed by what they and those around them are not doing to honor Jesus through the church.

No one has ever articulated the cost of discipleship so clearly, concisely, courageously, conclusively, and compellingly for me as a young African pastor who tacked the following declaration to the wall of his house:

MY COMMITMENT AS A CHRISTIAN

I'm part of the fellowship of the unashamed.
I have Holy Spirit power.
The die has been cast.
I have stepped over the line.
The decision has been made.
I'm a disciple of His.
I won't look back, let up, slow down, back away, or be still.

My past is redeemed, my present makes sense, my future is
secure.
I'm finished and done with
low living, sight walking, small planning, smooth knees, colorless
dreams, tamed visions,
mundane talking, cheap living, and dwarfed goals.

I no longer need pre-eminence, prosperity, position,
promotions, plaudits, or popularity.
I don't have to be right, first, tops,
recognized, praised, regarded, or rewarded.
I now live by faith,
lean on His presence,
walk by patience,
live by prayer,
and labor by power.

My face is set, my gait is fast, my goal is heaven, my road is
narrow, my way rough, my companions few,
my guide reliable, my mission clear.
I cannot be bought, compromised, detoured, lured away, turned
back, deluded, or delayed.
I will not flinch in the face of sacrifice,
hesitate in the presence of the adversary,
negotiate at the table of the enemy,

ponder at the pool of popularity, or meander in the maze of
mediocrity.
I won't give up, shut up, let up, until I have stayed up, stored
up, prayed up, paid up,
preached up for the cause of Christ.
I am a disciple of Jesus.
I must go till He comes, give till I drop, preach till all know, and
work till He stops me.

And when He comes for His own,
He will have no problems recognizing me –
My banner will be clear!

A woman who asked her doctor if the scar would show
at the beach after abdominal surgery comes to mind. He
answered, "That depends entirely upon you."

And the reality of our faith in private *and public* depends
entirely upon us.

Will it show?

He'll see.

SECRET 3

**People with *actual* authority over our lives are not *acknowledged*
as authority over our lives unless they are in consonance with
God's apocalyptic will exemplified in Jesus
and explained in the Bible.**

The most stupid people in the world are those who think they're smarter than God.

You know the kind.

They say things like, "I know that's what Jesus and the Bible say, but I think..."

They remind me of the celebrity on a late night talk show who gushed, "Well, well, well, that's enough about me. *What do you think of me?*"

Pathetically, the dominant *weltanschauung* of our culture is egocentric rather than theocentric.

Crudely, most folks don't get beyond navel-gazing in their search for truth.

That's why human institutions like government, media, organized religions, social clubs, and all the rest function as practical atheism; going about daily business with a wink to authority beyond auto-suggestion.

Bruce Ennis, a brilliant MIT graduated engineer, wrote one extraordinarily profound yet precise sentence on the inside back cover of his Bible on 14 November 1976 which he shared with me not long before going home to Jesus: "To any intelligent and perceptive human being exposed daily, as he is, to the beautiful miracles of this earth, and realizing that only some Power greater than he could produce such miracles, it must seem that an atheist has a low degree of intelligence, coupled with an abysmal lack of perceptivity, a deplorably egotistical self-esteem, and an unseemly arrogance."

Now that was one smart guy who knew God is smarter!

And looking at human history, we haven't been particularly proficient when left to our own sovereignty over things.

3/4 of the world is always at war.

The environment is going down the toilet quicker than poop through a goose.

Poor people starve to death as rich people fret over their quest to find a deodorant to keep them dry all day long.

Surfing cable television and the internet prove we're more debauched than ever.

Hosea was right: "There is no faithfulness...no knowledge of God in the land; there is swearing, lying, murder, stealing, and committing adultery...Therefore the land mourns" (see Hosea 4).

Maybe Darwin was right in *reverse*.

We're devolving into a planet of the apes.

There's more than enough evidence to prove we're not that smart.

We can't figure out how to live in peace and mutual concern.

How ironic that we've got so many institutions of higher education in our world yet remain such savages.

The problem was clarified for me many years ago by a gentle pastor near the Delaware Water Gap in New Jersey. He was my field education supervisor during seminary. As

I was asking him to review my course selections for the next semester, he stopped and seemed to plead, "Just don't separate yourself from God and His people *by degrees.*"

As the degrees piled up and years passed, I began to develop a distrust of the academic; noting how it encourages the egocentric over the theocentric.

I began to understand the cynicism of a college philosophy professor who many years before had lambasted me for participating in an egghead program: "You're a sorry bunch of ineffectual intellectuals who sit around all day in easy chairs assaying the human condition while offering no solutions to the hurting of this world."

I think he was saying we were full of _____ .

He echoed Clarence Jordan's paraphrase of 1 Corinthians 1:19-20 in *The Cotton Patch Version of Paul's Epistles* (1968):

> It's like the Scripture says: "I will tear to bits the dissertations of the Ph.D.s; I will pull the rug from under those who have all the answers." Then what becomes of the "bright" boy. What does this do to the "egghead"? Where does the worldly-wise professor wind up? Hasn't God made human reasoning appear utterly ridiculous?

It's like the Texan visiting an ivy league university. He asked a young student, "Excuse me, son, but can you tell me where the library's at?" The student turned up his nose and sniffed, "A Princeton man would never end a sentence with a preposition." "Excuse me, son," the long horn stater continued, "but can you tell me where the library's at...jerk!"

Brother Daniel, a monk at Ava, Missouri's Assumption Abbey, taught me how to become smarter about 20 years ago.

During a retreat at the monastery, I noticed the Trappist was reading Psalm 91 between duties. Emboldened by

Hebrew studies of the Psalm in Israel as well as Princeton, I felt obligated to enlighten him.

While telling him how much I knew about the Psalm, he seemed thoroughly underwhelmed.

So I asked him to tell me what he knew about it.

As he spoke through a warm smile and sparkling eyes, it seemed as if the heavens were opening and God Himself was communicating to me through this old monk who barely made it through 8th grade.

Finally, I asked, "How can you know so much more about this Psalm than me without the benefit of my education?" Brother Daniel smiled again and revealed the secret, "I asked God what it means."

If you want to know the truth, *go* to the source!

I can still talk and act as stupid as the next person; but now I know where to go for the smart answers to life's questions. God.

It's the most basic tool of Biblical exegesis.

Ask God what it means!

He should know.

He wrote it.

As Peter reported (2 Peter 1:20-21),

You must understand that no prophecy of Scripture came about by the prophet's own interpretation. For prophecy never had its origin in the will of man, but men spoke from God as they were carried along by the Holy Spirit.

Of course, it won't work if you stay stuck on yourself. That explains why there are so many stupid people in our world.

It has taken a very long time for me to recognize ability

42

and the authority to *engage ability* for the advancement of the Kingdom come from God alone.

God enables people to honor Him and help people on *earth as it is in heaven.*

Paul spelled out the specifics of God being the source of ability and authority (see Romans 12 and 1 Corinthians 12):

> **We have different gifts, *according to the grace given us*...There are different kinds of gifts, *but the same Spirit.* There are different kinds of service, *but the same Lord.* There are different kinds of working, *but the same God works all of them in all men.* Now to each one the manifestation of the Spirit is *given* for the common good.**

But when God's enabling is misused or misdirected, He recalls His authority.

It's Secret 3: "People with *actual* authority over our lives are not *acknowledged* as authority over our lives unless they are in consonance with God's apocalyptic will exemplified in Jesus and explained in the Bible."

There are some terrible misconceptions slithering around church and society about authority; as in *we should obey whoever is in charge.*

Lots of men feel that way; and they appeal to texts *out of context* like Ephesians 5:22-24: "Wives, submit to your husbands, as to the Lord. For the husband is the head of the wife...Wives should submit in everything to their husbands."

Lots of parents feel that way; and they appeal to texts *out of context* like Ephesians 6:1-2 and the fifth of the Ten Commandments (Exodus 20:12) as license to bully, boss, and abuse children: "Children, obey your parents in the Lord, for this is right...Honor your father and mother."

Lots of governments feel that way; and they appeal to texts *out of context* like Romans 13:1-7 and Titus 3:1 to justify their right to rule: "Let every person be subject to the governing authorities...Therefore whoever resists the authorities resists what God has appointed...be submissive to rulers and authorities."

Dictators in home, church, and society really like those texts *out of context.*

That's why Secret 3 is so important to digest.

It encourages us to consider all Biblical texts and claims to authority *within the context* of full Biblical revelation.

In other words, the whole is equal to the sum of its parts; but any one part should not be taken out of the context of the whole and mistaken for the whole.

Secret 3 reminds us of a fundamental rule of Biblical exegesis – study each text within the context of the whole Bible.

It emphasizes exegesis (pulling God's truth out of the text) over eisegesis (putting personal prejudices into the text).

Even the most cursory survey of the Bible reveals God does not affirm authority contradicting His character and expressed will.

God and the *Godly* have never instructed us to obey anyone who attempts to disobey Him, hurt people, or retard the advancement of His Kingdom.

That's why men have authority over our lives *as long as they are under the authority of God.* For if a man is under God, he will esteem his wife and edify his children: "Husbands, love your wives, as Christ loved the church and

44

gave himself up for her...Fathers, do not provoke your children to anger, but bring them up in the discipline and instruction of the Lord" (read all of Ephesians 5:22-6:4).

That's why governments have authority over our lives *as long as they are under the authority of God.* If a nation is under God as profiled in Jesus and prescribed in the Bible, then we are under it.

That's why parents have authority over children *as long as they are under the authority of God.* If parents are *under* God, they will lead their children along paths of righteousness.

The assumption of authority is submission to the authority of God in the exercise of authority over people.

It's very simple.

God is in charge.

God is head of the house, church, and society.

He is the *head Shepherd.*

All human authorities in consonance with His authority are undershepherds.

All human authorities are under the almighty authority of God.

And it is imperative to note, God exercises His authority in love.

Therefore, human authorities are validated by their love.

1 John 4:16 is the standard operating procedure for authorities: "We have come to know and to believe the love that God has for us. God is love, and whoever abides in love abides in God, and God abides in him."

The clearest apocalypse of God's love is Jesus.

God loves us best in Him (review John 3:16-17).

Therefore, anyone who asserts authority over our lives must wrap that claim in the love of Jesus; praying and laboring for our best as revealed in the person and proclamation of Jesus.

I think of the pastor who visited a large church in the redneck woods of the South.

He asked the hillbilly preacher, "How did you get the church this way?" "What way?" the preacher asked back.

"Well," observed the visiting pastor, "you've got a completely integrated church. There are rich and poor and black and white and yellow and red and brown in your church. Was it because of the Supreme Court decisions?"

The hillbilly declared more than asked, "What does the Supreme Court have to do with being a Christian?"

Good question.

The visitor persisted, "How did you get the church this way?"

Here's what the preacher said:

Well, our old preacher left our small church. After about three months without a preacher, I told the deacons, "I'll be the preacher!" So the first Sunday as the preacher, I opened the Bible and came upon these words: "For as many of you as was baptized into Jesus has put Him on. And there is no Jew or Greek or slave or free or male or female or anything else. You are one in Jesus." Then I closed the book. And I told 'em that when Jesus comes into your life, you become one with all kinds of people. And if you ain't, you ain't!

"What happened next?" the pastor asked.

"Well," he said, "the deacons took me into the back room after the service and told me they didn't want to hear that kind of preachin' no more."

"So what did you do?" he was asked.

"I fired them deacons!" came the resolute response.

Shocked yet pleased by that turn of events, the visitor asked, "Then what happened?"

And the faithful old hillbilly preacher reported, "I preached that church down to four. And then the church started to grow and grow and grow. And I found out that revival sometimes don't mean bringin' people in, but gettin' the people out who don't love Jesus."

Again, the assumption of authority is it is exercised by those *under* God.

That old hillbilly preacher knew his deacons had to be removed from office because they were not from, in, through, or for the Lord.

The same principle of authority is true for home, church, and society.

If anyone claims authority apart from God, they must be ignored; and if they cannot be ignored, they must be resisted.

Hitler, Hussein, and the like quickly come to mind.

When a woman or man or parent or government or church or anybody requires something from us which is contrary to the will of God as exemplified in Jesus and explained in the Bible, we must say with Peter, "We must obey God rather than men" (Acts 5:29).

Do you remember the Hebrew midwives? They are a perfect example of resisting unGodly authority (see Exodus 1:8-22):

Now there arose a new king over Egypt, who did not know Joseph. And he said to his people, "Behold, the people of Israel are too many and too mighty...let us deal shrewdly with them"...Then the king of Egypt said to the Hebrew midwives... "When you serve as midwife to the Hebrew women and see them on the birthstool, if it is a son, you shall kill him"...*But the midwives feared God and did not do as the king of Egypt commanded them, but let the male children live.*

It's the first commandment: "You shall have no other gods before me" (Exodus 20:3).

Or as Jesus said, "No one can serve two masters... You cannot serve God and mammon" (Matthew 6:24). And μαμωνα (mammon) is anyone or anything that distracts us from devotion to God!

In his *Confessions* (A.D. 397-400), Augustine noted the pre-eminence of God in all things at all times with all people:

But when God commands something contrary to the customs or laws of a people, it must be done, even if it has never been done before; if it has been neglected, it must be restored; and if it has never been established, it must be established...for it is a general law of human society for men to obey their rulers–how much more must God, ruler of all creation, be obeyed without hesitation in whatever he imposes upon it! Just as among the authorities in human society the greater authority is set above the lesser in the order of obedience, so God stands above all others.

Martin Luther put it this way in *To the Christian Nobility of the German Nation* (18 August 1520),

There is no authority in the church except to promote good. Therefore, if the pope... (or anyone) ...were to use his authority to prevent the calling of a free council, thereby preventing the improvement of the church, we should have regard neither for him nor for his authority...Let us, therefore, hold fast to this: no Christian authority can do anything against Christ.

John Calvin wrote in the *Institutes of the Christian Religion* (1536),

> Since the maintenance of His economy pleases the Lord God, the degrees of pre-eminence established by Him ought to be inviolable for us...that we should look up to those whom God has placed over us, and should treat them with honor, obedience, and gratefulness...Now this precept of subjection strongly conflicts with the depravity of human nature...the Lord therefore accustoms us to all *lawful* subjection...if they spur us to transgress the law, we have a perfect right to regard them not as parents, but as strangers who are trying to lead us away from obedience to our true Father. So should we act toward princes, lords, and every kind of superiors. It is unworthy and absurd for their eminence so to prevail as to pull down the loftiness of God. On the contrary, their eminence depends upon God's loftiness and ought to lead us to it.

But let's get really specific within the context of our contemporary church culture.

Most mainline denominations impose a *per capita* apportionment on their members. I say *impose* because apportionment is a euphemism for tax. Funds garnered through this apportionment are used for the administrative expenses of the particular governing body.

It makes sense.

It's kind of like paying dues to the Girl Scouts, Boy Scouts, Rotary, Kiwanis, Masons, Junior League, bowling league, and all the rest.

If you're going to claim the rights of membership in an organization, you've got a responsibility to help pay the bills.

Paul talked about that too (see 1 Corinthians 16:1ff.):

> **Now about the collection for God's people: Do what
> I told the Galatian churches to do. On the first day of
> every week, each one of you should set aside a sum
> of money in keeping with his income, saving it up, so
> that when I come no collections will have to be made.**

Yet, again, the assumption is the money will be used to honor God, help people, and advance the Kingdom as profiled in Jesus and prescribed in the Bible.

While I am fortunate to be in a presbytery (Blackhawk) or regional body of Christians in that part of the Kingdom called the Presbyterian Church (USA) which does a pretty good job of managing money for the glory of our Lord, many other churches in our denomination and others are not so blessed.

As one little boy said to his buddy, "My mommy said I can't go to church with you because we belong to different *abominations*."

Personally and prophetically, I cannot imagine any Christian giving money to anyone who does not honor God's will as exemplified in Jesus and explained in the Bible. For when we give money to anti-God organizations in church and society, we mock God's first commandment and the reality of Secret 1.

History will cite Joe Paterno as one of the greatest college football coaches. Though often criticized for making his players wear boring uniforms without names on them, his reasoning is persuasive:

> You folks miss the point. They are work clothes – *not dress
> clothes.* We are not out there to look flashy. It is a football
> game – *not a fashion show.* Secondly, we are a team –
> *not a collection of individuals.* Because we are a team,
> we don't single out any person or player. I know their
> names – *that is all that really matters.* Thirdly, *it is what
> is in a player's heart* – not on a uniform – that wins foot-

ball games.

I didn't know Coach Paterno was such a great theologian!

That's how God's team plays.

Jesus said, "Whoever does the will of my Father in heaven is my brother and sister and mother...My sheep hear my voice, and I know them, and they follow me" (see Matthew 12:46-50 and John 10:27).

Following God legitimizes authority.

Following God compels obedience.

Paul prodded (1 Timothy 2:1-4),

First of all, then, I urge that supplications, prayers, intercessions, and thanksgivings be made for all people, for kings and all who are in high positions, that we may lead a peaceful and quiet life, Godly and dignified in every way. This is good, and it is pleasing in the sight of God our Savior, who desires all people to be saved and to come to the knowledge of the truth.

Yes, we pray for all people.

We pray for our leaders and follow them as long as *they are under the authority of God* as exemplified in Jesus and explained in the Bible.

SECRET 4

**Trying to be rational with the irrational is illogical;
the ancillary being, *being wrong invalidates
argument and being right does not
necessitate it.***

When I was younger, I wanted to be older.

I couldn't wait until I was 16 so I could drive.

I couldn't wait until I was 18 so I could drink a beer as well as die in Vietnam.

I couldn't wait until I was 21 so I could be legal; though considering the behavior of my generation back then, I'm not sure why that was so important to me.

I couldn't wait until I was 25 so my insurance would go down before the next speeding ticket.

I couldn't wait until I was 30 because that's when I projected reaching all of my vocational goals; *which I did* only to discover I was leaning against the wrong building after climbing to the top of the ladder of ecclesiastical success.

I couldn't wait until I was 40 because that's when you're supposed to get your act together.

Dang!

Well, there's always 50!

A foul four-letter word ruined that for me.

AARP.

Now that I'm older, I want to be younger.

I get up to jog *and don't.*

I really, really, really like naps just *about anytime.*

I'd rather play golf than exercise.

And to think I thought going to the dentist and doctor was bad when I was a child.

It's hard to imagine that someone who still listens to Jimi Hendrix has ended up in audiences watching *About Schmidt*. It seems like only yesterday when wild horses dragging me by the tongue couldn't get me to watch *On Golden Pond*.

I'm starting to agree with the kid who told me that *adultery* is the sin of growing old.

He also said he had been watching old Lawrence Welk re-runs with *Pop-pop* and wondered if The Rolling Stones had ever been part of his stage band.

Yeah, I'm gassed about the passing of time.

But there is an upside to the downside of aging.

You can trust people over 30.

My good friend Jim Tuckett likes to say, "It is good for the young to be liberal; it shows they have heart. It is good for the mature to be conservative; it shows they have brains."

Or as my daddy likes to say, "A conservative is someone who doesn't like to see anything happen for the first time; and when you look at a liberal, you can't tell if she or he is having a vision of God or wetting themselves."

Nevertheless, you can trust the common sense of seniors because they've survived all of the nonsense for so long. That's a nice way of saying they have wisdom to share from bad decisions along the way that have made them that much wiser.

When you've been around for awhile, you can also look back and forward at the same time; building upon the best of the past for an even better tomorrow.

I'm convinced that's why seniors are so reliable in church and society. Recalling the past handed over to them, they invest in the future.

So when I'm told seniors are tight-fisted and resistant to change, I say they're *reasonable* and will open their pockets along with their hearts to anyone for anything that makes sense.

That's why I always expect older folks to turn out in large numbers to vote for tax increases in public education. They know no amount is too much to spend on our children who will be entrusted with preserving and promoting our best values.

Seniors understand the relevancy as well as religion of Deuteronomy 6:4-9 and Proverbs 22:6:

And these words that I command you today shall be on your heart. You shall teach them diligently to your children, and shall talk of them when you sit in your house, and when you walk by the way, and when you lie down, and when you rise...Train up a child in the way he should go; even when he is old he will not depart from it.

That's why I like seniors.

It's not just because I am one!

Though they're not getting any younger, they're old enough to know the best of yesterday for tomorrow depends upon what we're doing today.

Be that as it is, there's always someone whose bigotries, misconceptions, misrepresentations, illiteracies, ignorance, and the like confuse fiction with fact.

Instead of acknowledging the rules, they'll dwell on the exceptions.

Such irrational conjecture results in comments like these:

> *Old people long for the way things were and won't ever change.*
> *Young people have no sense of responsibility.*
> *It's just a guy thing.*
> *You know how women are during...*
> *Democrats have no morals.*
> *Republicans don't care about the poor.*
> *They're all alike.*

Have you ever considered all of the suffering caused by class, color, and culture caricatures?

There's too much truth in that *Hagar the Horrible* cartoon in which a monk says to the dimwitted barbarian, "I think therefore I am." Hagar's friend asks, "So where does that leave me?"

It's like the Texan, Russian, and New Yorker in a London restaurant. The waiter apologizes "Excuse me, but because of mad cow disease, we have a shortage of steaks." The Texan asks, "What's a shortage?" The Russian asks, "What's a steak?" And the New Yorker asks, "What's *excuse me?*"

Some people just don't get *anything.*

Because I do some writing, a friend thought I'd be interested in some *selected grammar rules* finding their way through cyberspace. Here are my favorites:

1. Verbs has to agree with their subjects.
2. Prepositions are not words to end sentences with (Remember?).
3. And don't start a sentence with a conjunction.
4. Avoid cliches like the plague. They're old hat.
5. Also, always avoid annoying alliteration.
6. Be more or less specific.
7. No sentence fragments.

8. Foreign words and phrases are not *apropos*.
9. One should never generalize.
10. Don't use no double negatives.
11. One-word sentences. Eliminate.
12. Never use a big word when a diminutive one would suffice.
13. Who needs rhetorical questions?
14. Exaggeration is a billion times worse than understatement.
15. Proofread carefully to see if you any words out.

Rosalie - Yes, the *same* Rosalie of Secret 2! - sent an appropriate illustration to me.

It's about two robins in a tree. They flew down to find something to eat. They ate so much that they couldn't fly back up into the tree. One said to the other, "Let's just bask in the warm sun." But as soon as they fell asleep, a big old tomcat pounced on them and gobbled them up. Afterward, the cat thought, "I just love baskin' robins."

Life is filled with irrational people and situations.

Have you ever tried Isaiah 1:8 - "Come now, let us reason together!" – with the scatterbrain piling two carts of groceries onto the *five items or less* express lane at the supermarket? If you did, Psalm 120:7 surely came to mind: "I am for peace, but when I speak, they are for war!"

How about dealing with that rude dude who just hopped out of the car and cut into line way up front after you've waited so patiently for your ticket to the latest *Star Wars* movie?

How about the reckless nutball who just veered into "your" cash *only* toll booth lane from five lanes over yet spends an eternity searching pockets, glove compartment, floor, seats, and ledge under the toll booth basket for the correct change?

Why is everybody in such a rush when you're not?

Why is everybody going so slow when you're running late?

Karl Barth, one of the most renowned theologians of Christian history, comes to mind.

You may remember how he responded to hearing that Pope Pius XII called him the greatest religious thinker since Thomas Aquinas: "Now even I can believe in the Pope's infallibility."

He's also the one who defined Christianity this way: "Jesus loves me! This I know! For the Bible tells me so!"

Questioned about his view on temperance, Dr. Barth quipped, "One may be a non-smoker, abstainer, and vegetarian, yet be called Adolf Hitler!"

Then there was the graduate student who asked, "What is the role of reason in your theology?" He responded, "I use it."

But if you're like me, you've run into lots of irrational people.

I'll never forget the elder who complained when I scheduled a female preacher during vacation. He was against women in the pulpit. He stated, "It's just not right!" When I referred to all of the great women of the Bible who proclaimed God's Word with Paul's endorsement like Phoebe and Priscilla (Acts 18:1-28; Romans 16:1-3), he huffed, "I still don't believe in them!"

He reminded me of the woman who scolded her pastor for mowing the lawn on Sunday. He reminded her of Jesus feeding the hungry on the Sabbath. She snapped, "Two wrongs don't make a right!"

There are moments in life and ministry when so overwhelmed by the irrational and irascible surrounding us that we are tempted to pray like the little boy who had just been scolded for something earlier, "I thank You, Lord, for preparing a table before me in the presence of my enemies."

Truly, sometimes it's better to talk to God about someone than to talk to someone about God.

It's Secret 4: "Trying to be rational with the irrational is illogical; the ancillary being, *being wrong invalidates argument and being right does not necessitate it.*"

Undeniably, we are called to love (αγαπη - agape) the irrational to irascible in our lives. Jesus expects us to pray and work for the highest good for others regardless of who, what, where, or when without the need or expectation of response, regard, or reward. We are to love 'em like Jesus loves 'em and remember loving them is how we love Him best. As He said, "As you do it for them, you do it for me" (see Matthew 25:31ff.).

Matthew 18:15-17 is our Lord's reconciling recipe for those irrational and irascible people in fighting moods.

I like Clarence Jordan's paraphrase in *The Cotton Patch Version of Matthew* (1970):

> If your brother does you wrong, go talk it out privately between the two of you. If he sees your point, you've won your brother. But if he won't see your side of it, take one or two others, since every fact, in order to stand, must have two or three witnesses. If he will pay them no mind, bring it up before the church. If he won't pay attention to them, chalk him up as a hopeless case.

Simply,

1. Try to work it out face to face.
2. If that doesn't work, bring along a few fair and objective folks who will tell the truth to both of you while insuring neither of you is tempted to lie about the conversation to

others at a later date.

3. If that doesn't work, try a committee, board, or bunch of good folks to sort it all out.

4. If that doesn't work, isolate and avoid 'em. Or as 8th graders say, "Just blow 'em off!"

Though our Lord commands us to love and seek reconciliation with even the unlovable people in our lives, He knows the response will not always be reciprocal. He knows some folks are just irrational and irascible.

There comes a time when we must *let go and let God* deal with them.

Paul pulled no punches (Romans 16:17-20; Titus 3:10-11):

I appeal to you...to watch out for those who cause divisions and create obstacles contrary to the doctrine that you have been taught; avoid them. For such persons do not serve our Lord Christ, but their own appetites, and by smooth talk and flattery they deceive the hearts of the naive. For your obedience is known to all, so that I rejoice over you, but I want you to be wise as to what is good and innocent as to what is evil. The God of peace will soon crush Satan under your feet...As for a person who stirs up division, after warning him once and then twice, have nothing more to do with him, knowing that such a person is warped and sinful; he is self-condemned.

Even our limitlessly loving Lord predicted some people will exhaust our best and most reconciling attempts (see Matthew 10:5ff.):

And whatever town or village your enter, find out who is worthy in it and stay there until you depart.

As you enter the house, greet it. And if the house is worthy, let your peace return to you. And if anyone will not receive you or listen to your words, shake off the dust from your feet when you leave that house or town.

Someone said, "Even in a world of dragons, our Lord has not given us permission to breathe fire."

Jesus offers no excuses or reasons for hitting back, getting even, and the like. He said, "Love your enemies and pray for those who persecute you" (see Matthew 5:43-48).

Hence, the second half of Secret 4 must be employed: "Trying to be rational with the irrational is illogical; the ancillary being, *being wrong invalidates argument and being right does not necessitate it.*"

Or as good old boys say, "Don't get into a tinkling contest with a skunk!"

I think of the note passed up to Dwight L. Moody while he was preaching. It had only one word on it: "Fool." The wise old evangelist looked at it for a moment or two and then said, "I've often received notes that weren't signed. This is the first time I've received a note that someone forgot to write, *but signed.*"

Jim Tuckett described too many relationships in his unpublished essay "Leadership and a Dead Horse":

The tribal wisdom of the Dakota Indians...says: "When you discover you are riding a dead horse, the best strategy is to dismount." However, in today's...businesses, ancient wisdom has been replaced by various advanced degrees. Some of our greatest academic institutions, boardrooms of our largest companies, and from committee reports of church boards have developed other strategies, including:

1. Buying a stronger whip.
2. Threatening the horse with termination.
3. Appointing a committee to study the horse.
4. Arranging to visit other sites to see how they ride dead horses.
5. Lowering the standards so that dead horses can be included.
6. Reclassifying the dead horse as living impaired.
7. Change the form so that it reads, "This horse is not dead."
8. Hire outside contractors to ride the dead horse.
9. Harness several dead horses together for increased speed.
10. Donate the dead horse to a recognized charity, thereby deducting its full original cost.
11. Providing additional funding to increase the horse's performance.
12. Do a time management study to see if lighter riders would improve productivity.
13. Declare that a dead horse has lower overhead and therefore performs better.
14. Promote the dead horse to a supervisory position.

Parenthetically, I think the preceding is why Jim left poverty-inducing pastoral ministry to become First Vice President for Morgan Stanley in Kansas City.

Putting it all together, I advocate *creative neglect* as the best approach to the irrational and irascible people in our lives.

Concisely defined within the context of the preceding, *creative neglect* is the practical application of κηρυσσω (*kerysso*) which is the most common Greek word for preaching or proclamation in the New Testament. Appearing 61 times in the New Testament (e.g., Mark 1:14; Acts 10:42; 1 Corinthians 1:23), it means "to cry out, to herald, exhort, announce, or declare." It is proclamation without proving, declaration without debate, and announcement without argument. It is telling the truth of God's will as profiled in Jesus and prescribed in the Bible without waiting around to entertain objections. Karl Barth once commented, "Preaching does not reflect, reason, dispute, or academically instruct. It proclaims, summons, invites, and commands."

Or as John Hall described the church's witness during the Lyman Beecher Lectureship on Preaching at Yale College in 1875, "Gentlemen, we are heralds, rather than logicians. We announce the Lord's will; many truths of the Word we may fearlessly declare without waiting to argue."

Creative neglect is proactive advancement of the Gospel in church and society unencumbered and undeterred by those who are not with Him.

Creative neglect considers cultural dissent to Jesus as irrelevant to its evangelistic and discipling responsibilities.

Creative neglect doesn't waste time or energy engaging the spiritually dark anti-God forces in church and society. It looks up, stands up, and speaks up for Jesus with all people in all places at all times without reference to the response.

The Confessing Church Movement in the Presbyterian Church (USA) is an example of Christians exercising *creative neglect* in response to an increasingly apostate denomination.

Instead of bantering and moaning about dissipating Christology and affronts to Biblical ethics, the movement upholds a simple statement of faith with three points as the foundation of its life and ministry:

1. Jesus is Lord and Savior.
2. The Bible is God's inspired rule for discipleship.
3. Christians are called to holiness as exemplified in Jesus and explained in the Bible.

Churches in the movement network with each other for encouragement and enabling, regarding those who do not share their confession as irrelevant to their commitment to clear, positive, proactive, and enthusiastic worship, work, and witness.

Instead of fighting with parts of the church, the movement prays and labors to *be* the church.

It's a salt and light thing (Matthew 5:13-16).

Creative neglect relieves the stress of fighting and replaces it with pressing forward with the Gospel.

It reminds me of Bert Atwood who used to tell his students at Princeton, "Trust Jesus and, in everything else, hang loose!"

Or as Dr. Bob Griffin, President of Rockford Renewal Ministries likes to say, "Haven't you heard of the 11th commandment? *Thou shalt not sweat it!*"

It's Secret 4.

SECRET 5

Knowing people get ticked off about almost anything anyway, tick 'em off on your terms; doing your best, intentionally and humbly, to bring your terms into consonance with God's apocalyptic will exemplified in Jesus and explained in the Bible.

You may have heard about the chicken who insisted on laying an egg in the middle of a busy street. A friend counseled, "If you're determined to do it, here's some advice: *do it quickly* and *lay it on the line.*"

That story reminds me of close friend Rus Howard.

Rus is the senior pastor of Peters Creek Presbyterian Church which is becoming an increasingly faithful congregation in the socioeconomically safe and serene South Hills of Pittsburgh, Pennsylvania.

Aside from being one of the most able, articulate, and persuasive pulpiteers in our franchise, he's an old school pastor whose genuine concern and call compel him to respond to the spiritual needs of anyone at anytime in anyplace.

He's not one of those 9 to 5 church professionals who limit their care and witness to 40 hours a week; making time for crises *when they get around to it* and showing up for a 2:00 a.m. hospital emergency as *soon as they can after lunch the next day.*

Rus is also a writer *with an edge.*

Because he understands ministry as encouraging and enabling the *Body of Christ* rather than a pay stub for rendered services, he's focused on how things *ought to be* in the church as profiled in Jesus and prescribed in the

Bible. He doesn't spend too much time on how things *never* were or maybe were but *may not be* anymore.

Convinced God's opinion matters most (Secret 1), he's not like those clergy who *agree with the last person they've talked* to and mouse around like the local *Good Humor Man* singing songs by Donny and Marie.

He's sold out to the Savior of souls which doesn't allow for saving his own skin for temporal securities.

In other words, he ticks off a lot of people.

Unfortunately, he's still got this commendably tragic naiveté of assuming people desire the truth even more than their emotionally, intellectually, and semi-spiritually inherited and conditioned prejudices.

I keep asking if he missed the course on original sin at Princeton.

Regardless, he experienced extended shock and sadness at receiving more than requests to be removed from his computer mailing list which carries the first editions of his essays, columns, quips, and so on.

His pain was compounded by a few less than charitable and sensitive sorts who clicked on the "Reply All" rather than "Reply" to *sender alone* command to register their disdain.

Though I'm computer-challenged like all card-carrying AARP members and praise God for Charles Pulliam of Greater Rockford's CompuDocs who keeps me on line with minimally enhanced pathologies, even I know "Reply All" sends one of two messages to my friend.

They'd like to *injure* him for saying what they don't want to hear or *ignore* him and pretend what they don't want to hear isn't being said.

They're either terrorists who spray their bullets

indiscriminately or ostriches who bury their heads from reality. Both are good but unsightly targets.

An apocryphal tale about President Bush seems analogous:

> President Bush encountered a man with long hair and a beard, who was wearing a white robe and sandals and holding a staff. He asked the man, "Aren't you Moses?" The man said nothing. Again, President Bush asked, "Aren't you Moses?" The man said nothing. So President Bush asked a secret service agent, "Doesn't this man look like Moses?" The secret service agent agreed, approached the man, and asked, "You look just like Moses. Are you Moses?" The man whispered to the secret service agent, "Yes, I am Moses. But the last time I talked to a bush, I spent 40 years wandering around in the desert!"

Nevertheless, such juvenile "Reply All" antics tempt me to the cynicism of Jack Nicholson's Marine Colonel Jessup in *A Few Good Men:* "You can't handle the truth!"

In a letter to friends who confronted a few critics, Rus appeared to be getting the bigger message:

> Thanks for coming to my defense when several folks have hit "Reply All" to ask that I remove them from my e-mails.
>
> I have granted all of their requests with two simple understandings.
>
> First, while many folks realize there are serious problems in the PCUSA, there are too many issues in their local churches which are consuming their energies. They just can't handle any more issues... While they cannot refute my statements, they can't handle the truth. Thus denial is the best avenue.
>
> Second, I suspect that some of these folks are hitting "Reply All" not because they disagree or dislike me, but because they want to distance themselves from me. Let's remember, in _____ Presbytery, there is one executive who

has told others that I will never get another call in Western Pennsylvania. When someone is being "black-balled," the best thing you can do is to distance yourself from them. I am not safe.

In my latest column, I did not say anything derogatory or harsh about anyone. In fact, it was a fairly mild column. I simply stated what we know is true...

Remember my last line: "People hate me because I want my old church back." Everyone I talk to wants their old church back. They simply are not willing to die for it.

There are so many dark spirits in our culture who conspire to *injure* others for saying what they don't want to hear:

☹ I talked to a church executive left of Dubuque who said pastors and parishioners who don't like what's going on in their denomination should just get out or be thrown out.

☹ I talked to a pastor right of Pittsburgh whose job security and opportunities have been threatened by a church executive who said he'd never allow that pastor to relocate in his jurisdiction because the pastor was *stirring up trouble* and not keeping quiet about problems in their denomination.

☹ After defending a young evangelical on the floor of Heartland Presbytery (Kansas City) many years ago, I was told by a church executive to forget *going anywhere in the denomination* because I refused to go along with *whomever* I was supposed to be accommodating.

There are too many pathetic spirits in our culture who want to *ignore* reality:

☹ The Three Stooges are being reincarnated in church and society. Too many are like *Curly* who cried out, "Moe! Moe! I can't see!" Moe asked, "What's wrong?" And

Curly answered, "I've got my eyes closed!" It's ostrich ecclesiology; pretending problems will go away if we don't acknowledge them. But when we pretend to see, hear, and speak no evil, that's when evil's grip tightens.

☹ A pastor who protested the dissipating Christology and Biblical integrity of_____Presbytery left to build a new church. The presbytery sent an executive to meet with the session. His first words: "You're going to get back to being Presbyterian. This is a Presbyterian Church first. Christian second." Silly me! I thought our faith was Christian and polity was Presbyterian!

☹ Talking with a predecessor in Kansas City, he said, "I live in the ambiguity of life." I quipped, "I'll bet that was a real help when you were pastor." He continued, "I ignore those *true believers* who are trying to change things." I asked, "Does that mean you stand by as people are bruised, beaten, and battered by evildoers? Does that mean you don't care about the lost in church and society?" He retorted, "I wouldn't put it that way." I pursued, "But what way are you putting it?" We never met again. Surely, innocuous is better than evil. But like abstentions in parliamentary order, it acquiesces to the majority for good or bad. Fence-sitters need to review Revelation 3:14-22.

☹ When PUBC (Presbyterians United for Biblical Concerns from the old Northern Church) and CFP (Covenant Fellowship of Presbyterians from the old Southern Church) negotiated to form PFR (Presbyterians for Renewal) after reunion in the early 80s, two pastors were asked to raise $50,000 each to provide $100,000 as the seed money for the new renewal organization combining the Northern and Southern counterparts. The money was raised with the expectation that PFR would build upon the prophetic as well as programmatic ministries of its predecessors. Indeed, the two pastors who were asked to raise the money along with many other prophetic voices during those nascent conversations were optimistic about a new wineskin to carry the Gospel to the franchise - a wineskin which would *be the church* in an increasingly apostate denomination increasingly anathema to the Kingdom of God and other evangelical/ecumenical denominations.

Surprisingly (?), the prophetic voices were never invited to participate in leadership because they were too "radical" in their approach and rhetoric. Talk about blood money!

Predictably, one of the fund-raising pastors left for another denomination and one stayed, sinned, went into the wilderness, and only resurfaced around 2000.

PFR continues to build upon the excellent discipling ministries of its predecessors; but lost its prophetic edge.

Today, it has lost the confidence of evangelicals as it appears too cozy with those contradicting Christianity as exemplified in Jesus and explained in the Bible.

Aside from parallel Secrets, Matthew 16:24-28 deserves another look.

Yet I may be as naive as Rus.

I still think most folks want to live righteously; and aren't afraid to entertain challenges to their prejudices as the salt that stings before it heals.

Most folks understand my friend's motivation as explained by Frederick Buechner in *Wishful Thinking* (1973): "A prophet's quarrel with the world is deep-down a lover's quarrel. If they didn't love the world, they probably wouldn't bother to tell it that it's going to hell. They'd just let it go."

Most folks agree with Grove City College Professor Earl H.Tilford: "Just because one hates to hear the message does not mean that the message is hateful...Ministers are called to lead their flocks toward righteousness...not to comfort in their sinfulness."

Most folks don't always *like* the truth; yet know they can't avoid it and must deal with it.

Consider Jesus.

Anybody who says everybody loved Jesus for what He said is betraying historical illiteracy.

He was nailed for telling the truth!

Or as Philip Yancey once remarked rhetorically, "How would telling people to be nice to one another get a man crucified?"

What government would execute Mister Rogers or Captain Kangaroo?

Invariably, I always cringe when a young Christian says, "I want to be just like Jesus."

Really?

Should we assume you mean without the cross?

Jesus ticked off lots of people.

He did that to move them from where they were to where they needed to be in Him.

He paid the consequences of telling the truth because He understood the path to existential and eternal freedom is truth. So if you're mousing to "Reply All" to avoid truth-tellers, take a moment to examine your motivations before questioning theirs.

One more thing.

Jesus loves you just the way you are; but He loves you too much to leave you just the way you are.

He's not the host of a children's show.

He is Lord.

He tells the truth.

So do those who love Him.

And just like Him, those who love Him will get into lots of trouble.

He warned, "You will be hated by all for my name's sake" (see Matthew 10).

He also counseled, "Woe to you, when all people speak well of you, for so their fathers did to the false prophets" (Luke 6:26). I like the paraphrase in *The Living Bible* (1971): "And what sadness is ahead for those praised by the crowds – for false prophets have always been praised."

Think about it.

If *everybody* likes you, that includes those who do not love and listen to Jesus as Lord and Savior.

If *everybody* likes you, that means you're all things to all people and not especially loyal to Jesus because your principles are relative to the cultural context. You *fit* in wherever and whenever with whomever. You're a spiritual chameleon. You're two-faced. You speak with *forked* tongue.

Let me tell you a secret.

Nobody trusts you.

Because sooner than later, people on different sides of the aisle get together and discover your allegiances and affections are only as good as your most recent contacts and conversations.

Being *liked* by *everybody* rarely, *if ever,* equates to faithfulness.

If we can't serve two masters, a handful or more is out of the question too.

Lamentably, too many Christians and churches in our culture are hypocrites; coming from υποκριτης *(hupokrites)* which means one who wears a mask to conceal true identity as in a pretender, deceiver, imposter, or fake.

There are too many anti-Christians or non-Christians diluting Christianity in the church these days.

There are too many folks wearing the mask but not heart of Jesus.

I think of the Pentecostal who went to a mainline church and later related to a friend, "That church was different. The only time I heard the name of Jesus was when the custodian fell down the stairs."

I was in Florida a few years ago because some guy took his church and pastor to ecclesiastical court; complaining they said he had to believe in Jesus to be an elder.

Imagine that!

O.K., that wasn't all.

They said he had to affirm the Bible as God's inspired rule for discipleship and try to be holy as profiled in Jesus and prescribed in the Bible.

Imagine that!

That's just one incident increasingly familiar in mainline denominations as they devolve to auto-suggestion rivaling divine apocalypse.

Hence, I have reached some harsh conclusions about too many "Christian" clergy, officers, and members: (1) Too many ignore Biblical faith when parts conflict with personal ideologies; (2) Some didn't understand the Biblical faith questions at membership or ordination; (3) Some lied and never really believed in Jesus as Lord and Savior or the Bible as God's inspired manual for life and ministry; or (4) Some changed their minds over the course of their lives and ministries and want their churches to honor

73

their disbelief if not endorse it.

Concisely, the church has a debilitating problem of hypocrisy.

An old Phil Donohue show before his second coming is almost revelatory.

A bunch of nuns were complaining about their church's pro-life position. A rabbi stood and said, "You knew what you were getting into when you took your vows. If you don't like it and can't change it, maybe you need to change or leave."

Imagine that!

The truth is Christianity is defined by the identity of Jesus as Lord and Savior and informed by the Scriptures of the Old and New Testaments as they witness to Him.

Therefore, **to be a Christian** is to pray and labor to say the things that Jesus would say and do the things that Jesus would do as understood within the context of Biblical Christology.

Admittedly, the answers don't always come easily; but asking the right questions – *What would Jesus say? What would Jesus* do? – lead us down the right road to the answers.

Let's experiment.

Let's ask some tough *Jesus* questions that will expose the truth of our Christianity:

- o Would Jesus gossip?
- o Would Jesus listen to rap music?
- o What would Jesus say about our giving to support the advancement of the Kingdom?
- o Would Jesus accept pedophilia, transexuality, homosexuality, promiscuity, adultery, "open" marriages, and other fashionable sexual identities as alternate lifestyles?

74

- Would Jesus perform an abortion?
- Would Jesus pull the switch?
- What do you think Jesus has to say about terrorists?
- Do you think Jesus would drop bombs on civilians to convince the really bad guys to give up?
- How do you think Jesus would react if he attended a school board meeting? Rotary meeting? Session meeting? You name it!
- What do you think Jesus has to say about your lifestyle?

Ouch!

That stings!

I better stop.

This game isn't any fun.

It's too *revealing*.

But those are the kinds of questions most appropriate for folks who claim to be His.

Sure, it hurts to ask those questions.

It hurts before it heals.

It's a *salt* thing.

Jesus said *salting* and being *salted* are a big part of discipleship: "You are the salt of the earth, but if salt has lost its taste, how shall its saltiness be restored? It is no longer good for anything except to be thrown out and trampled under people's feet" (Matthew 5:13).

The paraphrases of this text by Eugene H. Peterson (*The Message,* 1993) and Clarence Jordan (*The Cotton Patch Version of Matthew,* 1970) bring out the flavor of our Lord's instruction:

Jordan: "You all are the earth's salt. But now if you just sit there and don't salt, how will the world ever get salted? You'll be so worthless that you'll be thrown out and trampled on by the rest of society."

75

Peterson: "You're here to be salt-seasoning that brings out the God-flavors of this earth. If you lose your saltiness, how will people taste godliness? You've lost your usefulness and will end up in the garbage."

The value of salt (αλας - *halas*) in our Lord's day was an easy analogy for describing the positive and proactive qualities of discipleship: *preserving* who and what are good from going bad, *purifying* who and what have gone bad, and *flavoring* all relationships with the love and joy of Jesus.

Our Lord expects us to make that kind of difference in our world.

And that ministry often stings before it saves.

I think of it as Secret 5: "Knowing people get ticked off about almost everything anyway, tick 'em off on your terms; doing your best, intentionally and humbly, to bring your terms into consonance with God's apocalyptic will exemplified in Jesus and explained in the Bible."

Harold Mele, my good friend who served with me in ministry several years ago near Pittsburgh, was confronted by a woman at the beginning of a Bible study, "I am so angry with you for talking about me in last week's sermon." Harold said, "I don't recall mentioning your name." She said, "But I know you were talking about me." And sprinkling the salt that stings to heal, Harold remarked, "I know I wasn't thinking about you while preparing or preaching the sermon; but if the shoe fits..."

A friend once told Norman Vincent Peale, "You've got to take people as they are." Peale responded, "I don't believe that at all. I don't believe in taking people as they are. Take them as they can be, as they ought to be."

That's why Jesus salts us.

That why we salt the world and each other.

That's the redemptive reply to all.

SECRET 6

Pejorative instincts (aka *original sin*) require perpetual confession and repentance for redemptive dispensations.

Acknowledging my sin and dependence upon God's mercies for life and ministry, I always pray before preaching, "And now I pray, O Lord, that You will take this sin-stained life of mine, redeemed only through faith in Jesus, and work a miracle so that the words of my mouth and meditation of my heart may be acceptable in Your sight and to the glory and praise of Jesus alone in whose name I pray. Amen."

I used to beseech the Lord to "take my sin-stained *lips*" and all the rest until I asked Greg Apelian to open confirmation class with prayer at Osceola Presbyterian Church in Clark, New Jersey over two decades ago and he asked, "Should I start with your sin-stained lips?"

The class laughed in a markedly pubescent way that prompted a suitable synonym.

Actually, aside from church members who seem so *gifted* for humiliating clergy, the media and entertainment industries who make us look like buffoons or children of perdition, and a wife who always threatens to tell congregants what I'm really like after barking about *practicing what I preach,* I was sobered while overhearing a son say to classmates, "My dad is the best *sin*ister in town."

Honestly, while there are too many times provoking kinship to Paul's lament of being right down there among those who have most rejected God's will for their lives (see 1 Timothy 1:15), I know I'm neither as good as my mom pretends nor as bad as my antagonists advertise.

Paradoxically, I have found salvation in sin.

Before labeling me as a heretic, let me explain.

When I am conscious of my sins or how I am rejecting God's will for my life, I am driven to my knees in thanks to God for the gift of salvation through faith in Jesus even as I beg enabling to be more holy unto Him.

As Paul explained, "If it had not been for the law, I would not have known sin...Wretched man that I am! Who will deliver me from this body of death? Thanks be to God through Jesus Christ our Lord!" (see Romans 7).

Furthermore, when I am not aware of my sin, *then I am really under its spell.*

Self-ignorance is not bliss.

When we don't know we're out of step with the Lord, we're headed down life's wrong paths.

Putting it another way, you can't fix a problem until you know you've got one.

Hence, I am not as concerned about the sins that I'm confessing in profound penitence as much as the sins that have become such a part of me that I'm not aware of them and how they are crippling relationships with Him and His.

I think of it as emotional, intellectual, and spiritual numbness – the inability for *or disinclination to* self-awareness.

Contradicting the reality of personal sin, we assume innocence or blame others for provoking our pejorative behaviors; forgetting the truth relayed by Paul, "All have sinned and fall short of the glory of God" (Romans 3:23).

I detected this numbness in me again upon hearing

about the deaths of seven astronauts as the space shuttle Columbia disintegrated on 1 February 2003.

On my way to preside at a memorial service after emergency marital counseling with thoughts obsessing about pastoral concerns piling up juxtaposed to family needs, I called my dad around 9:15 a.m. (CST). Immediately, he asked if I had heard about the space shuttle. Not having heard about the disaster which occurred only about an hour earlier, he supplied available details.

After hanging up and continuing to drive to the funeral home, I turned on the radio and listened to breaking news.

Aside from recollections of Challenger's unforgettable explosion on 28 January 1986 and thoughts turning to the immediate grief of families who were minutes away from reunion with loved ones returning from outer space, I found myself so preoccupied with a day's personal agenda that I was somewhat numb to the whole thing.

Or maybe in a world lingering after 9/11 and close to another world war, it was "just another" unspeakable horror on an expanding list; causing such an overload of pain that I was becoming numb to all of it.

I'm not sure.

But I'm concerned.

I've got this nagging notion that being numb to pain in this world isn't a long leap from being numb to pain being caused by me.

Again, I'm not sure.

But it's worth self-examination because self-awareness is always the first step to salvation from sin.

That's why churches are so big on confession.

As a preacher, I handle our Lord's pure and perfect

Word in Jesus as attested by the Bible with dirty hands.

Though God's saving grace in Jesus to forgive through faith is always the ultimate exclamation of faithful homiletics, I confront sins in church and society as a mirror reflecting true identities.

An underlying goal is exhorting to confession (acknowledgment of sin) and repentance (turning from sin to righteousness) for redemption (a restored or "saved" relationship with God which yields confident living in the assurance of eternal life).

It's a saving equation:

confession + repentance = redemption.

I look at our world and see the incarnation of Hosea 4:

> **Hear the word of the Lord, O children of Israel, for the Lord has a controversy with the inhabitants of the land.**
> **There is no faithfulness or steadfast love, and no knowledge of God in the land; there is swearing, lying, murder, stealing, and committing adultery; they break all bounds, and bloodshed follows bloodshed.**
> **Therefore the land mourns...**

Then the prophet notes the etiological culprit:

> **Yet let no one contend, and let none accuse, for with you is my contention, O priest...**
> **My people are destroyed for lack of knowledge; because you have rejected knowledge, I reject you from being a priest to me. And since you have forgotten the law of your God, I also will forget your children.**

Hosea placed the blame for the plethora of insults to God's holiness at the feet of clergy; the assumption being clergy are supposed to be heralds of holiness with a message as simple as the old gospel song that goes, "Trust and obey, for there's no other way to be happy in Jesus, but to trust and obey."

A few thousand years later, I'm convinced blame can still be placed at the feet of clergy; especially mainliners.

Trying not to be too sarcastic about their annual meetings looking like a Ray Stevens Shriners' Convention in which any connection between Jesus and them is coincidental or invoking the shocking statistics of their accelerating downward spiral to oblivion making mainliners nothing more than sideliners in American religious life with the transforming impact on society of a Faith Hill video, anyone who suggests the old mainline denominations are nothing more than holding tanks for pulpiteers and pewsitters longing for the way things never were or maybe were but are no more must be having flashbacks from before the 60s.

Fortunately, the recent movement of mainliners from museums of spirituality to mausoleums of theological uncertainty at best or duplicity at worst makes little difference to the ultimate triumph of God's Kingdom. As Jesus assured, "I will build my church, and the gates of hell shall not prevail against it" (Matthew 16:18).

Mainliners have lost so many members over the past four decades that they're quite insignificant players on the national and world stages. Nobody seems to notice them and very few movers and shakers listen to them as they fade into lesser obscurity.

My franchise, for example, has lost nearly 2 million members since 1965 (PCUSA); though in amusing irony, more bureaucratic and para-denominational booths pop up in the exhibition halls of our annual meetings as membership plummets.

Many observers assert a connection between decline and the dissipation of core confessions: (1) Jesus is Lord and Savior; (2) The Bible is God's inspired rule for discipleship; and (3) Depending upon God's grace, we are called to holiness as profiled in Jesus and prescribed in the Bible.

Denominational revival is envisioned as plausible with a clear, consistent, courageous, enthusiastic, and unequivocal commitment to such confessions.

Or as an older elder said to me many years ago, "Watch the birds! They go where there is food!"

And *you can't give away what you ain't got for yourself!* That's the real problem with today's mainliners.

As Hosea wept, "There is no knowledge of God in the land."

I'm convinced the decline of the mainliners can be attributed to unconverted clergy, unconvinced laity, and pharisaical reincarnations substituting organizational order for Biblical authority:

Unconverted clergy or women and men without faith infect every level of church life. They are easy to identify. Talking about Jesus by name is onerous for them. If you aren't sure about this, approach a suspect and ask her or him to say a few words about personal faith in Jesus. Ask for commentary on Romans 10:9. I have never experienced anyone who believes in Jesus who isn't psyched to talk about Him.

Unconvinced laity are the children of unconverted clergy. It's the old *shepherds don't follow sheep* axiom. Sadly, to borrow a line from Margaret Thatcher, "Standing in the middle of the road is very dangerous; you get knocked down by traffic from both sides." Obviously, mainline laity are sheep without shepherds (Isaiah 53:6). With undershepherds (clergy) misunderstanding the *Good Shepherd* (Jesus) through confessional confusion, sheep (members) are like two mainliners at fellowship hour. One says, "I don't know who I am or where I'm going." The other says, "Don't worry about it! Our pastor is going through the same thing!" Getting back to the real issue, John Eldredge identifies the problem and provides the solution in one sentence: "Healing never happens outside of intimacy with Christ" *(Wild at Heart,* 2001).

Pharisaical reincarnations substituting organizational order for Biblical authority explains how mainliners can violate Biblical ethics on everything from the sanctity of all human life to human sexuality so blithely. Assuming the Bible is not bigger than their favorite parts, they embrace an ethical relativism which enslaves all issues of faith and morality to the most recent popular vote. Apostasy is acceptable as long as parliamentary procedure is used. No wonder missionary and seminary professor Samuel Moffett bellowed at the Presbyterian Congress on Renewal in Dallas, Texas (January 1985), "I've had decency and order up to here! But where's the power?...Where's the power to propel us across the world?...Some of the most creative and effective periods in the Church were those periods when the Gospel was hot and not respectable."

Time is running out for mainliners.

Here's why: "I have this against you, that you have abandoned the love you had at first. Remember...from where you have fallen; repent, and do the works you did at first. If not, I will come to you and remove your lampstand" (Revelation 2:1-7).

Many observers believe the lampstand has been removed already from mainliners.

In a letter addressing the unspoken reality of all mainline denominations, a lawyer (former pastor) wrote,

"Is the PCUSA simply old wineskins that must be abandoned? Or is there a sense of corporate forgiveness and redemption for past sins? It's one or the other. It cannot be both. If it's a wineskins problem, don't waste your time trying to reform. Get out! But if God truly is redemptive and forgiving, He can give these gifts to the organization."

I'm not sure.

If our lampstand or *efficacious place in the Kingdom* hasn't been removed, it's flickering, fading, and failing.

That's why I often suggest efforts to *renew* the mainliners represent bad stewardship; because you can't renew something that has not been *newed.* It appears we need to be *reborn* rather than renewed.

But when I preach the pure and perfect Word of the Lord and really go after sin in others, I recall a cartoon in a newspaper about 35 years ago in which a pastor says, "And at this time our hearts go out to all those pure and perfect newsmen who search for sin in others."

And I hear the Lord asking again, "What's that I see in your eye?" (see Matthew 7:1ff.).

Though I claim Christianity's redemptive ethic for myself – "It doesn't matter where you're coming from; all that matters is where you're going!" (Brian Tracy) – I am mournfully aware (Matthew 5:4) of how I have hurt too many people in the process of insulting God's holiness by contradicting Christianity in too much of my confession (what I say), conduct (what I do), countenance (how I appear), and conscience (what I think about right and wrong).

Yes, I agree with the saint who said, "I don't have to remember who I was; because that wasn't me anyway."

Yet I am sorry for past sins that compromised the integrity of my witness.

While I rejoice in personal redemption of Biblical proportions (see John 3; Acts 9), I comprehend if not appreciate anyone who wants to discredit who I am by referring to who I was.

Finally embracing the saving equation for myself - confession + repentance = redemption - I fessed up a few years ago with a rather detailed personal testimony:

"A broken and contrite heart, O God, You will not despise..."
Psalm 51

"Do not think of yourself more highly than you ought,
but rather think of yourself with sober judgment,
in accordance with the measure of faith
God has given you."
Romans 12:3

"Blessed are those who mourn, for they will be comforted."
Matthew 5:4

There's an old song by Neil Young that goes, "My life is changing in so many ways. I don't know who to trust anymore. There's a shadow running through my days like a beggar going from door to door."

Finally, I think I understand those lyrics.

That's why I'm making my public confession; believing tools of darkness include anonymity, secrecy, hypocrisy, and self-righteousness.

It's said confession is good for the soul but bad for your reputation; but considering reputation has been the greatest stronghold of sin in my life for too many years, I'm ready to sacrifice it. I'm not concerned about my confession's play in darkness or even how it can be manipulated by darkness because I have been compelled by our Lord to do this for Him, my wife and sons, parents, sister, friends, franchise, and anyone who needs to know the redemptive ethic of Christianity is more than theory.

My life came full circle as I was moving to the end of a half-century.

When I was called into pastoral ministry for the first time while strolling Princeton's campus with my pastor The Rev. Harold F. Mante in 8th grade, all I wanted to do was talk about and live for Jesus; inviting and enabling others to share His unconditional love.

While any connection between that nascent call and my character has surprised me as well as others on too many occasions, I have never doubted my call or gifting.

Indeed, my gifting has been one of the problems throughout my life and ministry. Or better said, my stewardship of the gifts has been less than sterling.

Sadly, I used my gifts to satisfy self-absorbed professional goals; achieving all of them by 30. But once I had climbed to the top of the ecclesiastical ladder of success, I discovered I was leaning against the wrong building.

My downward spiral into sin commenced (accelerated) when called as senior pastor to a very large church at a very young age; and though our Lord used the mismanaged gifts entrusted to me in spite of me, I was going to hell figuratively *and literally.*

A few comments about my life prior to accepting that call are in order.

Before entering college, I made a lot of mistakes not atypical to children of the 60s. That soon faded as I discovered scholarship and intellectual facility.

I *married* in my senior year of college. Well, I *kind of* married. Hindsight has helped me to understand her as a very decent woman who has tried very hard to be a good mother to our three sons. Unfortunately, the chemistry wasn't appropriate and we went our separate ways. She met a fine young man who complements her quite well; and my wife came into my life.

Succinctly, apart from Jesus, my wife is our Lord's greatest gift to me. Regrettably, like my other gifts, I was not a good steward of our marriage; particularly between February - April 2000.

Before going any further, this is my confession. Mitigating circumstances and contexts coupled with the culpabilities of others are no longer relevant to me. I have been compelled by our Lord to *own* my own sins and let others *own* theirs. Though I am especially tempted to reveal all I know about others to soften this confession in a twisted the-best-defense-is-a-good-offense manner especially regarding a few folks who cannot own their own sins and failures and hide behind pretended purity and innocence while pointing to my sins, I do not believe that serves any redemptive purpose. Aside from personal revelation on this decision, I will not say anything about anyone for my advantage. I only want and pray God's best for them. I have done this for a long time now with more success than failure by the grace of God. I am more determined *and called* to this intercession than ever before.

And I'd also like to thank our Lord for His continuing favor, my wife for her unrelenting call to be my wife, my family, friends, two executive presbyters, and a psychiatrist and psychotherapist who unmasked the real enemies within. Their combined love and energy delivered me from emotional, intellectual, physical, and spiritual illness that threatened everything that has always been important to me. I know who I can trust. I trust God through them.

Shadows.

Though I connect with the apostle (Romans 3:23; 1 Timothy 1:12-17), two shadows run through my days. Until I had completely confessed and repented, these shadows were leading me to the edge of emotional, intellectual, physical, and spiritual suicide. Seemingly endless mourning in the context of Psalm 51 and Matthew 5:4 kept me on my knees; which is where I need to be daily.

As my *marriage* to the mother of my three older sons was crumbling, I found temporal succor with another. I could not detach myself from the relationship for many years. I reveled in the excessive affirmation and affection; but as I began to recognize the transparency of the relationship, I tried to pull away. I did not tell her to back off and go away; not because I loved her, but because I feared she would betray our previous tryst of years ago. I liked her personally and prayed release from her and for her regularly. Because I was afraid of what she would say about the past and how it could taint my reputation, I feigned reciprocity. I pretended romantic intentions while I wanted friendship; though romantic expressions had ceased for at least 15 years. Fearing friendship wasn't enough for her, I sinned in continuing the charade of some future relationship.

In the late 90s, our marriage had reached a very vulnerable stage. Coupling familial, physical, vocational, and psychological dysfunction, I reached out to an extended hand. I confessed the sin to my session within weeks and began intense therapy; being diagnosed with a bipolar disorder which I now suspect bordered on schizophrenia. The healing process was arduous.

God knows I know I said some things that I never should have said. I made some comments over the telephone that were particularly bizarre and out of character. Upon hearing them, I felt ashamed by the rambling and barely coherent blubberings of a lovesick pup. And while my mind is blank on other possibilities related to that fast and furious relationship, I assume the worst.

Her husband orchestrated an investigation with my presbytery. Before meeting with the committee, an officer of the presbytery came to my home and urged me to lie to save my ministry and family's security. When I said I would confess what I knew – spiritual adultery at a minimum – I was told my personality and witness had not won many friends in the presbytery. In other words, the encouragement to lie was reiterated strenuously. I did not lie; but, then again, it was a very sick time in my life.

I was surprised by two things about the committee. First, they went far beyond their prerogative of the immediate charge and dug up all the real and imagined dirt available since ordination; confirming the concerns of the officer. Second, they concluded there was not enough evidence to file charges against me; yet they excoriated me for conducting ministry in a way that encouraged distractions and misinterpretations. Their concerns and counsel have been helpful.

These shadows surface in my life every now and then through bad memories, dreams, personal mourning, and folks who bring them up for different reasons.

Spiritually, I thank God for these shadows as His continuing chastening instrument (Proverbs 3:11-12).

I thank God for the healing that has come into my marriage, family, and ministry since being born *anothen* in the middle of 2000.

For the first time in my life, I have *freedom* through, in, and for Him.

I am unquestionably more effective and fulfilled as a husband, father, son, brother, friend, pastor, and presbyter than ever before.

Depending upon God's grace, I have decided to be His in all things at all times in all places with all people.

I praise and thank God for these redemptions.

Yet I know I have insulted our Lord's holiness in the shadows of the past, hurt my wife and family and friends and church by rolling along on gifting for so long without getting help because of that dark stronghold of reputation; and cooperated with at least two folks who may have meant well for me but were misguided by their own demons and my intentions.

Hence, my celebration is muted by constant intercessions for healing in lives adversely affected by me over the years and personal petitions and increasing spiritual discipline to maintain and increase the redemptive realities since being born *anothen.*

My love for and from my Lord, wife, sons, parents, sister, family, friends, and others have given me the freedom to confess my sins and encourage everyone who reads this to increase holiness in honor of our Lord and as the most effective way to avoid the aforementioned pain.

If you haven't done it already, I beg you to confess your sins to Jesus and invite Him into your heart right now to experience His salvation; because it will honor Him as it spares you from the horrible pains of unholiness.

I pray God's redemption in your life.

And I know you can experience *Him* through confession and repentance right now.

I have a friend who said to me not long after being born *anothen*, "It's time to start acting forgiven and redeemed. The time for mourning has passed."

Now I can. I do.

My joy in Jesus grows daily.

While I doubt I will ever stop mourning completely, I have finally claimed and experienced the mercy of God for myself which I have always been so quick to grant on His behalf since that stroll in 8th grade.

My freedom is becoming so complete in the Lord that I am eager to share this testimony for His glory alone with the hope that it will inspire anyone living in the shadows to move into His light.

Light always clears up the darkness.

There is no fear in love. But perfect love drives out fear... Everyone born of God overcomes the world. This is the victory that has overcome the world...Who is it that overcomes the world? Only he who believes that Jesus is the Son of God...He, who has the Son, has life...
1 John 4-5

I have developed an abbreviated testimony worksheet to help believers share their faith in four simple sentences;

knowing we've got to be clear, concise, and conclusive when someone asks about our faith (cf. 1 Peter 3:15):

1. Before I knew Jesus as my Lord and Savior, I was...
2. Jesus became a part of my life when...
3. Now that Jesus is a part of my life, I am...
4. If I could leave you with one thing, it would be...

Just to show you how it goes, here's my abbreviated testimony:

1. Before I knew Jesus as Lord and Savior, I was disappointed, depressed, oppressed, and a lousy husband, father, son, brother, and caught up in the "polity" correctness of being a mainliner.

2. Jesus became a part of my life when I became conscious of my sins, confessed them, and realized my need for rebirth even though I'd been playing the role for almost 30 years.

3. Now that Jesus is a part of my life, I feel whole, happy, joyful, secure, and generally psyched about life; and I think I'm a much better husband, father, son, brother, herald, pastor, and presbyter.

4. If I could leave you with one thing, it would be to invite Jesus into your heart and get with Him in worship as soon as possible; unless, of course, you're one of those really sick people who like being miserable.

That's how easy it is to share your faith with someone. And remember the old missionary's urging, "The only Gospel some people will ever hear or see is the Gospel *according to you.*"

Realistically, this does not mean being born *anothen* equates to perfect obedience.

I confess I've sinned since then.

I share the human condition of inherited sinfulness or natural proclivity to reject God's will for my life over and over and over again.

Paul noted the common problem of humanity in himself (see Romans 7):

I do not understand my own actions. For I do not do what I want, but I do the very thing I hate...It is no longer I who do it, but sin that dwells within me...I have the desire to do what is right, but not the ability to carry it out. For I do not do the good I want, but the evil I do not want is what I keep on doing. Now if I do what I do not want, it is no longer I who do it, but sin that dwells within me.

Then finding salvation in sin, he exclaimed, "Wretched man that I am! Who will deliver me from this body of death? Thanks be to God through Jesus Christ our Lord!"

Undeniably, sinning is in our genes.

We sin quite naturally.

As David admitted, "I was born in iniquity; and in sin did my mother conceive me" (see Psalm 51).

We call it the doctrine of *original sin.*

Simply stated, it is the label given to our inherited instinct to believe and behave in ways that offend and insult God's holiness. It refers to the cause and continuing cancer of humanity's natural propensity to contend with divine imperatives. It laments personal choice over the will of God – the subordination of God's sovereignty to self-interest.

It goes backs to the garden (see Genesis 2-3) when God told Adam and Eve what He expected ("Don't eat that fruit!") and our first parents did what they wanted ("Have some, honey!"). They blew off God like teenagers blow off their parents and did their own thing.

That was the original *or first* sin.

And there has been nothing original about sin ever since.

We're the Adamsons - the daughters and sons of Adam and Eve; and as everyone knows, the apple doesn't fall far from the tree! Donald G. Bloesch defined it in *Essentials of Evangelical Theology* (1978): "Original sin is not a biological taint but a spiritual contagion which is nevertheless, in some inexplicable way, passed on through biological generation."

A. Elwood Sanner summed it up quite neatly (*Beacon Dictionary of Theology,* 1983):

> Original sin in the exact sense is man's first transgression of God's law. In a more general sense, original sin is often defined as "the universal and hereditary sinfulness of man since the fall of Adam"...Original sin has also been described as "the human self corrupted, diseased, fevered, or warped – a condition brought about by alienation from God."

"Original sin," wrote John Calvin in *Institutes of the Christian Religion* (1536), "seems to be a hereditary depravity and corruption of our nature, diffused into all parts of the soul, which first makes us liable to God's wrath, then also brings forth in us those works which Scripture calls 'works of the flesh.' "

The Scots Confession of 1560 outlines the effects: "By this transgression, generally known as original sin, the image of God was utterly defaced in man, and he and his children became by nature hostile to God, slaves to Satan, and servants to sin."

It's no wonder an old Pentecostal preacher shouted, "I

don't talk about backslidin' no more 'cause most folks don't get far enough ahead to slide back!"

We call it total depravity in Reformed Theology; the inability to save ourselves from inherited and perpetuating sin along with the recognition of reliance upon God's grace to do for us what we cannot do for ourselves (i.e., secure salvation).

Surely, after two thousand years of salvation history, we know we are *saved* from the consequences of sin for eternal life and confident living because of Jesus. Paul wrote (see Romans 5),

> **God shows His love for us in that while we were still sinners, Christ died for us...We have been justified by His blood...Just as one man's trespass led to condemnation for all [Adam], so one man's act of righteousness leads to justification and life for all [Jesus].**

Calvin was precise: "Adam was...the root of human nature... implicating us in his ruin, destroyed us with himself; but Christ restores us to salvation by His grace."

I have never heard or read anything better on overcoming *original sin* and our *total depravity* through faith in Jesus than John Jasper's sermon "Where Sin Come From?" Here are sermon excerpts from the former slave who went on to distinguish himself as one of America's greatest preachers after his *rebirth* - the hard-drinking preborn Jasper went through four wives before his 27th birthday! – and emancipation:

And you want to know where sin come from...

The Bible say that Eve was over there in the garden of Eden one day and that she was there by herself. The Lord made Eve, 'cause it weren't good for Adam to be alone, and it looks from this case that it was not quite safe for Eve to be left at home by herself. But Adam weren't with her; doan know where he was...He better been at home tendin' to his family...

While Eve was saunterin' and roamin' aroun' in the beautiful garden, the ole serpent, dyked up to kill, come gallivantin' down the road and he catched sight of Eve...Now you mus' know that ole serpent was the trickiest and the arties' of all the beas' of the field...And what he do but go struttin' up to Eve in a mighty friendly way, scrapin' and bowin' like a fool dead in love...

"How you do?" He tries to be polite, and puts on his sweetes' airs. Oh, that was an awful moment in the life of Eve and in the history of this poor lost world of ours. In that moment the poison eat through her flesh, struck in her blood, and went to her heart...

"Nice garden you got there," he say in er admirin' way... "Can you eat all the apples you got over there?"

"No, indeed," says Eve, "we can't eat 'em all. We got more'n we can 'stroy save our lives"...

"Oh, I didn't mean that... My point is, is you 'lowed to eat 'em all?"

"What you ask me that question for?" Eve asked..."The Lord He tell us we mus' not eat them apples; they poison us, and the day we eat 'em we got to die"...

"Did the Lord God tell you that? Doan tell nobody, but I want to tell you that it ain't so. Doan you believe it. Doan let Him fool you! He know that's the bes' fruit in all the garden – the fruit of the Knowledge and the Distinction, and that when you eats it you will know as much as He do. You reckon He wants you to know as much as He do? Na-a-w; that's why He say what He do say. You go get 'em. They's the choicest fruit in the garden, and when you eats 'em you will be equal to God."

Alas, alas! Poor deluded and foolish Eve! It was the moment of her everlastin' downfall...That deadly day she broke 'way from the God that made her... and partook of the fruit that brought sin and ruin and hell into the world...

After a while, Adam come walkin' up the garden and Eve she runs out to meet him. When he come near she hold up her apple in her hand and tell him it is good to eat...First deceived herself, she turn roun' and deceives Adam. That's the way; we gets wrong, and then we pulls other folks down with us...

But where was the wrong?...It was in Eve's believin' the devil and not believin' God. It was doin' what the devil said and not doin' what God said.

And you come here and ask me where sin come from? You see now, doan you? It come out of the pit of hell where it was hatched 'mong the angels that was flung out of heaven 'cause they disobeyed God...It was brought by the ole serpent, the father of lies, and he bring it that he might fool the woman, and in that way set up on the earth the works of the devil...It come from the ole serpent at first, but it's here now, right in poor Jasper's heart and in your heart; wherever there is a man or a woman in this dark world in tears there is sin – sin that insults God, tears down His law, and brings woes to everybody...

But this is enough. I just took time to tell you where sin come from. But my tongue can't refuse to stop to tell you that the blood of the Lamb slain from the foundation of the world is greater than sin and mightier than hell. It can wash away our sins, make us whiter than the drivin' snow, dress us in redemption robes, bring us with shouts and hallelujahs back to that fellowship with our Father, that can never be broken long as eternity rolls!

Or as Paul reminded the faithful, "Nothing can separate us from the love of God in Christ Jesus our Lord" (see Romans 8:31ff.).

We are related to Adam and Eve through our parents and through their parents and through their parents and so on right back to the garden.

The bad news is we're the Adamsons; rejecting God's will for our lives so naturally.

The good news is God's grace through Jesus provides the spiritual detergent strong enough to remove sin's stain from our souls.

So it's true.

I'm not O.K.

You're not O.K.

But God says, "I love you anyway!"

It's like a friend says,

> I sin.
> God saves.
> What a great deal!

But lest we be tempted to *sin boldly that grace may abound*, which is another way of saying so cavalierly that it's easier to ask forgiveness than permission, eternal salvation from sin does not eliminate the terrible existential consequences of sin.

A story comes to mind:

Every time a farmer's son did something wrong and asked for forgiveness, the father offered total pardon. He asked his son to do only one thing: "As far as I'm concerned, you are totally forgiven. But here, take this hammer and this nail. I'd like you to drive this nail into the barn door and leave it there."

Whenever the son asked for forgiveness, the father gave forgiveness; but always handed him a hammer and a nail.

The son always followed the instructions.

Finally, the son asked, "Why do you keep telling me to pound those nails into the barn door?"

The father answered, "Before I answer, I want you to go and pull out all those nails and bring them back to me; telling me what you saw."

When the boy came back with the nails, he said, "The door is filled with nail holes."

And the father said, "That's the way it is with sin. It leaves its scars. It has its consequences. My forgiveness is total. But sin still has its results."

Gary Collins wrote (*Christian Counseling,* 1980), "We serve a God who forgives even though the scars...may remain a lifetime. If we confess any sin we are forgiven, but then we have the obligation to change our subsequent behavior to make it consistent with the Scriptures."

Thankfully, our sins are not being *saved* on the hard drive of His book of life.

But whenever we sin, our lives become a lot harder in the meantime.

That's why somebody referred to churches as local chapters of *sinners anonymous.*

We've always got that temptation to sin.

We're addicted to sin.

And the only way to get off that road to ruin is to *turn to* the *right*eousness of God.

It's like Junior told Bunny in *Platoon* (I'm paraphrasing), "Free your mind and your butt will follow."

That's the counsel of Hebrews 12:2: "Let us *fix* our eyes on Jesus."

Jesus pronounced the reward: "If you abide in my word, you are truly my disciples, and you will know the truth, and the truth will set you free" (John 8:31-32).

When we turn to Him, we are saved.

It's that simply saving equation:

confession + repentance = redemption

It's Secret 6: "Pejorative instincts (aka *original* sin) require perpetual confession and repentance for redemptive dispensations."

I guess that's why Christianity has always been so easy to sum up.

Two words.

Jesus saves!

SECRET 7

**Borrowing a line, "It is better to light a candle
than curse the darkness."**

Dr. Robert A. Amon, head of oral surgery at Rahway Hospital in New Jersey, walked into my study in Clark's Osceola Presbyterian Church about 25 years ago to discuss and pray about his vocational crisis.

I had come to know Bob as an extraordinarily evangelistic elder; which is rare among mainliners. He was so outspoken about Jesus that we called him *oral* Robert.

For example, every Easter Day, he would throw open his bedroom window at the crack of dawn and yell to his neighbor, "Barry, Jesus is risen! He is Lord! And He loves you, friend!" Barry would yell back, "I know because you keep telling me!"

I'll never forget sitting in the chair seconds before he pulled out a wisdom tooth. He asked, "Would you like to pray before I start?" I said, "Listen, Bob, if we have to pray about this, I'm outta here!"

Seriously, he was always passing out Gospel tracts and Jesus bumper stickers, arranging for busloads to attend those big Jesus rallies in football stadiums in the middle to late 70s, and bringing in guest speakers for church breakfasts and dinners and special services who talked so much about Jesus and the gifts of the Holy Spirit that people began talking behind his back about how he'd gone off the deep end. It wasn't uncommon for someone to ask, "Why doesn't he just quit his job and get a church?"

103

That's why Bob came to see me.

He talked about wrestling with call as a freshman at Rutgers University. Though feeling called into pastoral ministry, he knew there would be more money in medicine. He joked about there being no need for Protestant clergy to take a vow of poverty because congregations keep them in it. So he went on to become one of the most respected and successful oral surgeons in Union County.

About 25 years later, he was still wrestling with his decision.

After reviewing Romans 12 and 1 Corinthians 12 which articulate the equality of value in the diversity of vocations, we prayed for a very, very, very long time.

Being much younger and bolder, I suggested as he left, "Well, you're almost 50. If you're ever going to do it, you better do it now. Why don't you go to seminary and see what happens?"

Not long after that, he sold his business and was admitted to Princeton Theological Seminary. He was called as an associate pastor of the First Presbyterian Church of Southport, Indiana after graduation and spent his entire ordained pastoral ministry there until retirement about two years ago.

While speaking at Tabernacle Presbyterian Church in Indianapolis, Indiana on 19 January 2003, I spotted him in the congregation. After a brief chat, we arranged for lunch the next day.

Sitting together after so many years, I was warmed and stirred once more by his passion for Jesus.

I asked forgiveness for failing to stay in touch.

Then I told him how I had been born *anothen* about three years before and now understood his past and continuing fervor.

I even confessed being a little skittish about his witness and less than always supportive when we were at Osceola.

It was almost as if I were seeking absolution.

The mentor had become the student.

He said, "I'm so overjoyed to see the new person. I had heard about it. But I had to see it. That's why God sent me to see you last night. Listen, you weren't as bad as you want to confess; and you know I did the same things before I came into your office so long ago. Hey, I was your age back then! Now look at me! God can use anybody who lets go and lets Him! Welcome back, brother!"

I take away four lessons from that divine appointment spanning a quarter of a century.

First, an authentic rebirth in Jesus fuels unparalleled joy.

Second, an authentic rebirth in Jesus restores relationships thought to be lost.

Third, no matter who you are or how old you think you are, you're still young enough to be called into new adventures of service.

Fourth, we have been entrusted with the privilege of pointing people to Jesus by creed and deed as accomplices in enabling salvation.

Jesus had us in mind when He charged, "You are the light of the world...let your light shine before others, so that they may see your good works and give glory to your Father who is in heaven" (Matthew 5:14-16).

If our Christianity is authentic, all of us become *oral* Roberts.

I've always liked this line from William Shakespeare: "How far that little candle throws his beams! So shines a good deed in a naughty world."

Or as somebody said, "When the sun shines through the windows of a barn at a new day, the birds sing *and the rats run for cover.*"

It's Secret 7: "Borrowing a line, 'It is better to light a candle than curse the darkness.'"

Instead of spending so much time on what's wrong in the world, it's better stewardship to invest our energies in *showing* (example) and *telling* (exhortation) people how to get better by getting right with God.

I think it was C.S. Lewis who said he didn't spend much time telling people that they're going to hell because he thought it made more sense concentrating on telling them how to get to heaven.

Francis of Assisi agreed: "All the darkness in the world may not extinguish the light of a single candle."

One of the primary functions of Christians is *lighting up* the world.

We *show* and *tell* people the better way - *His way* as profiled in Jesus and prescribed in the Bible.

We *reflect* the light of the Father (see 1 John 1:5) and the Son Jesus (see John 8:12; 9:5) who charged as He complimented, "*You* are the light of the world."

What an incredible compliment!

God is light, *Jesus* is light, ...and *we* are light!

We are *Christians* or little *Christs* – representations of Jesus in the world.

What an incredible charge!

We are expected to be and do what Jesus was and did.

We are to become increasingly like Jesus and mirror His ministry.

106

Paul put it this way (Romans 12:1-2; 2 Corinthians 3:18; 4:5-7):

I appeal to you therefore, brothers, by the mercies of God, to present your bodies as a living sacrifice, holy and acceptable to God, which is your spiritual worship. Do not be conformed to this world, but be transformed by the renewal of your mind, that by testing you may discern what is the will of God, what is good and acceptable and perfect...we...are being transformed into the same image from one degree of glory to another. For this comes from the Lord who is the Spirit...What we proclaim is not ourselves, but Jesus Christ as Lord, with ourselves as your servants for Jesus' sake. For God who said, "Let light shine out of darkness," has shone in our hearts to give the light of the knowledge of the glory of God in the face of Jesus Christ. But we have this treasure in jars of clay, to show that the surpassing power belongs to God and not to us.

Specifically, we are to *shine* for Jesus, *show* the way to Jesus, and be *saving* partners in ministry with Jesus.

We are to shine for Jesus.

I like Eugene H. Peterson's paraphrase of Matthew 5:14-16 in *The Message* (1993):

You're here to be light, bringing out the God-colors in the world. God is not a secret to be kept. We're going public with this, as public as a city on a hill...By opening up to others, you'll prompt people to open up with God, this generous Father in heaven.

Commenting on this text, Matthew Henry said we must be "illustrious and conspicuous" about our discipleship.

Whoever said we're supposed to keep our religion to ourselves hasn't read the Bible. The good news of Jesus is for everybody. He said, "For God so *loved the world...*" (see John 3:16-17). It's absolutely antithetical to everything we know about God's love for the world to keep Him all to ourselves.

Parenthetically, I am convinced people who spew out such Biblically and Christologically ignorant nonsense are only trying to rationalize their inability and unwillingness to talk about a faith unpossessed by them. Their knowledge of and relationship with Jesus are so minimal that they don't have anything to say about Him. Or to repeat the old Pentecostal, "You can't give away what you ain't got for yourself!"

Christianity is not a secret society. We don't have secret handshakes or passwords or access codes or any of that other juvenile backyard playpen exclusionary stuff. It's easier to to get into the Kingdom than secure a tee-time at Rockford Country Club. That's why Jesus told us to shine: "A city set on a hill cannot be hidden. Nor do people light a lamp and put it under a basket, but on a stand, and it gives light to all in the house. In the same way, let your light shine before others..."

There's a story of a Roman soldier who approached Julius Caesar for permission to commit suicide. The man appeared miserable, mean, and mad. Sizing up the man quickly, Caesar asked, "Man, were you ever really alive?"

I have a friend who urges people not to pray, "And if I should die before I wake..." He believes they should pray, "And if I should *wake* before I die..."

*Christians are meant to be **seen!***

*Christians are meant to **shine!***

That's why we don't sing, "Sit down, sit down for Jesus...We don't have a story to tell to the nations...And they'll know we are Christians by our silence...Go, keep it a secret on the mountain...Lord, I want to be a Christian in my heart and make sure nobody knows about it...Take the name of Jesus with you but don't tell anybody else..."

We are to show the way to Jesus.

When I was a little boy, I never went into the attic or basement without a flashlight. I wanted to know where I was going; and I wanted to be sure I didn't end up in the wrong place.

Christians do that for people.

Christians point people in *His* direction.

Bob Amon preached about Christians showing the way to Jesus on 15 September 1985:

God has given every single Christian person the mandate to be a teacher for Him...

God has made it clear that all Christians are responsible to teach Christianity. Each one of us teaches by example - by our lifestyle. How does the world see us? How does our child or spouse see us? How do the members of the church see us? What are we teaching them about Christianity by our actions? Do we teach "love thy neighbor" by the way we drive?

When I gave my life to Jesus Christ and became a Christian, I was so excited and so on fire that I wanted to let the world know I was a Christian. I wanted to put Christian bumper stickers on my car. But all of a sudden, I realized I couldn't. Why? Because I didn't drive like a Christian. I practiced driving like a Christian for one year before I put those bumper stickers on. Now I've got them on the front and the back because I want to take every opportunity to teach something about my Lord. It really amazes me how people will plaster all kinds of bumper stickers on their cars to teach things to people like so and so is running for mayor or Disney World is great for kids, or you can get more gusto with Schlitz or even such great information as honk if you're horny. But it also amazes me how few Christians want to teach something to people like *Jesus - Your Only Passport to Heaven,* or *Jesus is Lord,* or *Get Hooked on Jesus.*

Christians are not designed to be distractions, detours, discouragements, or disillusionments from the Savior. We are to show the straight paths to the Savior.

We are saving partners in ministry with Jesus.

I was interviewing a candidate for ordination in our franchise not too long ago. He is very bright; and after four years of college and almost three years of seminary, his cumulative grade point average hovers near 4.0. But after listening to him for nearly three hours, I was astounded by how much he had to say about everything and everyone but Jesus. So I said, "Friend, I don't know how you expect to ever communicate the love of Jesus to anyone if you can't talk about His place in your life after three hours reviewing your call to ministry."

I'm reminded of the psychiatrist who was asked by a young mother when she should begin teaching values to her daughter.

The psychiatrist asked the age of the little girl. When told she was almost three, he said, "Hurry home as fast as you can! You're already three years late!"

Jesus said, "As long as I am in the world, I am the light of the world" (John 9:5).

Now that Jesus the Son reigns with God the Father in heaven, it's our turn to shine and show the way to salvation as enabled by the Holy Spirit.

We're like the ace reliever on a baseball team. In these late innings, our Lord Jesus has tossed the ball to us and said, "Here, pitch!"

I was in the Mayflower Restaurant with Steve Strickler, a good friend and staff member for pastoral relations of the Presbyterian Lay Committee, on 4 February 2003.

As we walked into the restaurant, I noticed a big table of folks who seemed to be having a really good time together. Noticing a few Bibles sprinkled here and there, I asked what had brought them together. When they said they were part of a local church's Bible study, I said, "I hear that members of your church really believe in Jesus."

Unlike mainliners who would feign insult while emitting scarce traces of faithfulness, they started smiling and yapping and clapping and radiating the joy of Jesus in their lives.

Steve asked if I do that kind of thing very often.

I said I haven't been able not to do that kind of thing since being born *anothen*.

When you've got a personal relationship with Jesus, you *light up!*

I learned that from *oral* Robert a long time ago.

It's like that old camp song goes, "If you're happy and you know it, then you really ought to *show* it."

When we *shine* for Jesus and *show* the way to Jesus to express our saving partnership with Jesus, God the Father, Son, and Holy Spirit is glorified.

SECRET 8

While never underestimating *poneros*, never doubt Jesus as *kurios* of all.

Evangelism is a word almost as scary as *Jesus* to mainliners.

We know that because it, like Jesus, rarely passes through their lips.

While former seminary professor and moderator of the PCUSA George E. Sweazey often referred to evangelism as "the greatest work in the world," it's one of those *practices* that publicly proper religionists like mainliners relegate to sideliners who purportedly roll and spit in the aisles during worship.

Isn't it odd how some labels lose their meaning?

Mainliners used to refer to the old familiar denominations like Episcopalians, Lutherans, Methodists, Presbyterians, and the like who were the backbone of religious life in America. They were strong advocates of Biblical fidelity and Christocentrism; growing in numbers and sociopolitical influence.

Sideliners were under-educated and Emily Post-impaired folks like Pentecostals, charismatics, evangelicals, fundamentalists, "Holy-rollers," non-denominationalists, independents, and others who didn't appeal to American Christians in large numbers *until the last three decades or so.*

Today, the sideliners have become the real mainliners by virtue of their continuing Biblical fidelity and Christocentrism complemented by stunning growth in membership, financial wherewithal, and sociopolitical clout.

The reason for this shift is as simple as the explanation offered to me by an older elder in a Greensboro, North Carolina diner about 20 years ago, "Watch the birds! They go where there is food!"

I'm convinced Christians want to hear more about Jesus and what it means to follow Him than the humanistic ideologies being parroted in mainline pulpits without reference to constitutional and confessional standards provoked by Biblical and Christological revelation.

I'm convinced mainliners don't talk much about Jesus because they don't know Him well enough to have much to say about Him. It's hard to make Him known without knowing Him personally as Lord and Savior.

I'm convinced mainliners don't quote the Bible as their rule for faith and morality because they don't really believe it is the inspired revelation of God; besides, it too often contradicts their carnal instincts which are confirmed extra-Biblically.

I'm convinced Jesus is Lord of all; and all who love Him as Lord pray and labor to become more like Him in confession (what they say), conduct (what they do), countenance (how they appear), and conscience (what they think).

I'm convinced the Bible is bigger than our favorite parts; showing us the best ways to honor the Lord, help people, and advance the Kingdom in *profession* and *practice*.

You can argue with such rationale; but you cannot argue with the reality of mainliners moving to the sidelines of religious life in America.

You can argue with the merits of this shift in numbers and influence; but you cannot argue with the reality of the old mainline denominations' declining relevancy in America.

Excuses, contentions, and intellectual apologies do not change a basic axiom of organizational life–*you get better or you get worse but you don't stay the same.*

Unless you're like France and Germany whose navel-gazing and sinisterly selfish interests regarding hosts of international terrorism with frightful amnesia about their historical vulnerabilities (France) and culpabilities (Germany) in the 30s and 40s have blinded them to the need for proactivity rather than *wishing problems away* or *trying to be rational with the irrational* (Secret 4), you can *see* more than *sense* the old mainline denominations are very ill.

Sociologists are telling us to make funeral plans.

Back in the 70s when the inevitable extinction seemed less probable, I was a younger pastor assigned to the evangelism committee of Elizabeth Presbytery (central New Jersey).

I'll never forget when we planned to host a major evangelism conference for the Synod of the Northeast (all of the presbyteries in New England). We spent lots of time, energy, and money on guest speakers, workshops, supplies, arrangements, and all of the rest.

I was the registrar. That meant I counted heads, and helped project the eventual attendance.

A few weeks before the conference, I asked the chairman (Dwight White), "How many people do you think are coming?" He responded, "No matter how many come, the conference will be successful. The people who show up will be the ones who God wanted to show up."

He taught me that success for a Christian is measured by nothing more or less than faithfulness to God. If the *practices* of our *profession* are pleasing in God's sight, we are successful. Nothing but God's opinion matters *in the end.*

Therefore, we do our best and trust Him for the rest.

Though knowing we are partners in ministry with Him, the ultimate triumph of His Kingdom depends more on Him than us.

Or as Jesus trumpeted, "I will build my church, and the gates of hell shall not prevail against it" (Matthew 16:18).

That's good to remember when we're feeling too full of ourselves; as if the Kingdom rises or falls on our efforts.

That's good to remember when we're too down on ourselves, mainliners, sideliners, and all of the below; as if the Kingdom rises or falls on our efforts.

It's healthy and humbling to know we can help our Lord to establish His Kingdom while not being necessary to the ultimate success of His creating, sustaining, and saving ministries.

He is, *before all* and *above all* and *after all,* Lord!

That's the good news of Matthew 16:18.

God wins *with* or *without* us.

No one nor no thing can defeat Him.

"The Church's One Foundation" (S.J. Stone, 1886) declares,

The Church's one foundation is Jesus Christ her Lord;
She is His new creation by water and the word:
From heaven He came and sought her to be His holy bride;
With His own blood He bought her, and for her life He

116

died...
'Mid toil and tribulation, and tumult of her war,
She waits the consummation of peace for evermore;
Till with the vision glorious her longing eyes are blest, And
the great Church victorious shall be the Church at
rest...

Regrettably, there's always been some confusion about Matthew 16:18. William Barclay noted it "is one of the storm-centers of New Testament interpretation...for it is the Roman Catholic foundation of the Pope and of the Church" (*Matthew,* 1956).

The particular assumption by our Roman Catholic friends is this text exalts Peter as the foundation of the Church.

The whole notion of the Roman Catholic Church's pre-eminent place in the Kingdom as *mother church* is tied to Peter being the first bishop of Rome by virtue of Jesus' designation in this text; thereby assuming apostolic position, power, prestige, and pre-eminence to whomever succeeds Him in Rome from then forward.

Let's take a closer look at the first half of this text which has been at the center of this ecclesiastical storm: "And I tell you, you are Peter, and on this rock I will build my church..."

Even the most elementary exegesis of Matthew 16:18 dispels the fiction of Rome's claim.

This text is an apocalyptic play on words in which two distinct words for *rock* are used to illustrate the substantial difference between Peter as disciple (Πετρος- *petros* which means *little rock* or *piece of a large rock)* and Jesus as Lord (πετρα- *petra* which means *large rock* or *bedrock).*

Pointing at Peter, Jesus said, "You are *petros*." Then

117

pointing at Himself, Jesus said, "And on this *petra* I will build my church." Paraphrasing a bit, it went like this, "You are rock solid, Peter; and on me, the rock foundation, I will build my church." Putting it another way, comparing Christians to the Christ is like comparing BB guns to heavy artillery.

Substantially, there is no comparison.

He alone is divine with Father and Spirit.

Using the same word (πετρα- *petra)* for rock to emphasize Jesus as the one and only foundation of the church, Paul wrote (1 Corinthians 3:11; 10:1-4),

For no one can lay a foundation other than that which is laid, which is Jesus Christ...I want you to know, brothers, that our fathers were all under the cloud, and passed through the sea, and all were baptized into Moses in the cloud and in the sea, and all ate the same spiritual food, and all drank the same spiritual drink. For they drank from the spiritual rock that followed them, and the rock was Christ.

The Greek is unmistakable.

Christians like Peter are helpful, but *Jesus is necessary.* Using the same word (πετρα- *petra)* for rock, Jesus pressed the point in the conclusion of His *Sermon on the Mount* (Matthew 7:24-27):

Everyone then who hears these words of mine and does them will be like a wise man who built his house on the rock. And the rain fell, and the floods came, and the winds blew -and beat on that house, but it did not fall, because it had been founded on the rock.

But as my grandpa Jacob Kopp used to say, "Don't miss

the forest because of the trees."

Differentiating the majors from the minors or what's important from what's incidental is the key to emotional, intellectual, and spiritual maturity.

For example, whether a church uses oil-filled, electric, or all-wax candles is infinitely less important than celebrating and worshiping Jesus as the *Light of the world.*

Indisputably, while Peter's role in the early church was helpful, the entire witness of the New Testament echoed in this text is Jesus alone is necessary for the church's empowerment, endurance, and eternity. This text is hardly as concerned with Peter's role in the church as disciple as our Lord's sovereign role which insures the church's indestructibility.

The message is as basic as this familiar chorus:

He is Lord!
He is Lord!
He is risen from the dead and He is Lord!
Every knee shall bow, every tongue confess that
    Jesus Christ is Lord!

Or as my favorite goes,

Praise the name of Jesus,
Praise the name of Jesus.
He's my rock, He's my Fortress, He's my Deliverer,
In Him will I trust.
Praise the name of Jesus.

While deferring to God's sovereignty on all matters of life and eternity including divine predestination over human volition, John Calvin sounded a warning even in his hopeful comment on this text (*Institutes of the Christian Religion,* 1536):

It is a promise...that all who are united to Christ, and

119

acknowledge Him to be Christ and Mediator, will remain to the end safe from all danger...*Yet this passage also instructs... that so long as the Church shall continue to be a pilgrim on the earth, she will never enjoy rest, but will be exposed to many attacks; for, when it is declared that Satan will not conquer, this implies that he will be her constant enemy. While, therefore, we rely on this promise of Christ... this promise is...calling us to be always ready and prepared for battle.*

After confirming the comforting message of Matthew 16:18 which declines the ability of all dark forces combined to frustrate the inevitable reign of God, he predicts the shifted focus of Satan from our unconquerable Lord to us because we are *human* enough to be discouraged, disillusioned, distracted, detoured, deterred, devastated, and destroyed.

With this in mind, Jesus taught us to pray, "Deliver us from the evil one" (Matthew 6:13).

Jesus our Lord God Almighty (κυριος- *kurios*) taught us to ask to be rescued from the evil one (πονηρος - *poneros*).

Not only recognizing the presence of dark forces in our world, Paul also pinpointed their driving source (see Ephesians 6:10-20):

For our struggle is not against flesh and blood, but against the rulers, against the authorities, against the cosmic powers over this present darkness, against the spiritual forces of evil in the heavenly places.

I like the paraphrase of J.B. Phillips in *The New Testament in Modern English* (1958):

For our fight is not against any physical enemy: it is against organizations and powers that are spiritual. We are up against the unseen power that controls

this dark world, and spiritual agents from the very headquarters of evil.

Just as one must dig deeper than the hands of a broken watch to find out what's wrong, Paul digs deeper to identify the source of all dark and evil energy.

Though it's easy to blame the hands, we must dig deeper for the head. Instead of targeting the *willing* and *unwitting* accomplices of darkness, we must take the battle to the source.

It's like the old priest said to his younger colleague in *The Exorcist* after the suggestion of several demons possessing the young victim, "There is only one!"

Or as William Hendriksen wrote in *Ephesians* (1967), our enemy is "the devil himself and all the demons under his control."

Helmut Thielicke preached in Stuttgart, Germany during the last days of World War II, "Behind the temptations stands the tempter, behind the lies stands the liar, behind all the dead and bloodshed stands the 'murderer from the beginning' " (*Our Heavenly Father*, 1960).

Paul said we are being attacked by "all the flaming darts of the evil one" (Ephesians 6:16). Or quoting Phillips again in a surprisingly forecasting paraphrase when considering it was written almost 50 years ago, we are being attacked by "every burning missile the enemy hurls at you."

Again, Jesus fingered the real enemy as πονηρος *(poneros)* - the *evil one;* which we know to be Satan.

The Biblical names for Satan betray the character of *the evil one.* He is called *Satan* which means *adversary* or *opposing spirit; devil* or *slanderer; Beelzebub, the prince of demons; Belial* or *the low one; that old serpent; god of this world; prince of this world; prince of the power of the air; dragon; accuser of the brethren; father of lies;* and the like.

Jesus said, "He was a murderer from the beginning; and has nothing to do with the truth, because there is no truth in him...he is a liar and the father of lies" (John 8:44).

Clearly, we have a formidable foe.

"If he were not so dangerous," Dr.Thielicke emphasized, "then surely Jesus would not have taught us to pray for deliverance from him."

Martin Luther assessed the supernatural strength of our real enemy in "A Mighty Fortress Is Our God" (1529): "His craft and power are great, and armed with cruel hate, on earth is not his equal."

Luther lectured on him as "the clever trickster": "But in the spiritual area, Satan emerges...in the guise of an angel or even God Himself." Or as the Rolling Stones sang, "Confusing is my game. Can you guess my name?"

The facility for confusion and deception to seduce is highlighted by Satan's use of the Bible. Just as Satan quoted the Bible to tempt Jesus away from divine intentions (see Matthew 4:1ff.), he will twist Biblical truth for his own purposes; taking texts out of context for inappropriate confirmation of evil intentions.

Unquestionably, Satan's greatest trick is to convince people that he doesn't exist; for if we are not aware of this sneaky son of Sheol slithering around to wreck havoc in our lives, then we are especially prone to falling into his traps. Problems are compounded when we don't think they exist. Richard Lovelace commented in *Renewal as a Way of Life* (1985),

> "Hell is a conspiracy," as Whittaker Chambers once said, "and the first requirement of a conspiracy is that it remains underground." If "the god of this world has blinded the

minds of unbelievers, to keep them from seeing the light of the gospel of the glory of the Messiah" (2 Corinthians 4:4), then he is surely capable of pulling the wool over the eyes of Christian intellectuals and whispering in their ears that he does not exist.

John Calvin outlined Satan's schemes:

For he opposes the truth of God with falsehoods, he obscures the light with darkness, he entangles minds in errors, he stirs up hatred, he kindles contentions and combats everything to the end that he may overturn God's Kingdom and plunge men with himself into eternal death.

An older pastor told me how to distinguish the light of the Lord from the darkness of Satan many years ago:

God does not want to tear us down, pick us apart, burn bridges, fracture families, degrade, denigrate, devastate, or destroy us.

That's the work of Satan.

God builds bridges, relationships, friendships, families, and reconciles, heals, helps, includes, invites, enables, elevates, enlightens, and encourages.

Satan says, "You're no good. You're bad. You're useless. You don't belong."

God says, "Come to me." God invites and includes. God loves.

Satan's strategies can be summed up in one prefix: *anti*.

Satan is *anti*-God. Satan is *anti* anyone or anything honoring God's will as expressed in Jesus and the Bible: *anti*-faith, *anti*-creation, *anti*-life, *anti*-conversion, *anti*-forgiveness, *anti*-redemption, anti-family, *anti*-marriage, *anti*-mission, *anti*-compassion, *anti*-mercy, *anti*-joy, *anti*-peace, *anti*-patience, *anti*-kindness, *anti*-goodness, *anti*-humility, *anti*-self-control, *anti*-love, and all the rest.

Satan targets our vulnerabilities.

Denise Frangipane cautioned, "Satan is a master of illusions. He plays upon our weaknesses and exaggerates our problems...Satan's strategy is to come at us when we are most vulnerable" (*Deliverance from PMS,* 1992).

If your marriage is weak, he'll send a Jezebel - *and they come in male as well as female enfleshments* - to seduce you into sin.

If you're low on money, he'll provide an opportunity to steal. If you're being abused at work, he'll push you to abuse at home. If you've been hurt, he'll provide somebody to hit.

If you've got any problems from the past, he'll present occasions to repeat them.

If you like to play with fire, he'll make sure you're burned.

His reason for being is to beat up and break down God's people; distracting them from knowing Jesus as Lord and Savior *better* and getting *better* at making Him known to people who need Him so desperately.

That's the bad news.

Now here's the good news from James on how to fight back: "Submit yourselves therefore to God. Resist the devil and he will flee from you. Draw near to God and He will draw near to you" (4:7-8).

Using the metaphor of a Roman soldier preparing for battle, Paul prescribes the specific battle plan and gear for defeating Satan (Ephesians 6:10-20):

Finally, be strong in the Lord and in the strength of His might. Put on the whole armor of God, that you may be able to stand against the schemes of the devil...Take up the whole armor of God, that you may be able to withstand in the evil day, and having done all, to stand firm. Stand therefore, having fastened on the belt of truth, and having put on the breastplate of righteousness, and, as shoes for your feet, having put on the readiness given by the gospel of peace. In all circumstances take up the shield of faith, with which you can extinguish all the flaming darts of the evil one; and take the helmet of salvation, and the sword of the Spirit, which is the word of God, praying at all times in the Spirit, with all prayer and supplication.

Andre Bollier, a friend and member of Kansas City's Second Presbyterian Church, wrote as a young man in his early 20s, "If we think that we have within ourselves the strength to overcome evil, we are in for an unpleasant surprise."

Henri Nouwen put it this way in *The Way of the Heart* (1981):

> The task is to persevere...until all my seductive visitors get tired of pounding on my door and leave me alone...Anyone who wants to fight his demons with his own weapons is a fool...The wisdom of the desert is...to surrender ourselves totally and unconditionally to the Lord Jesus Christ. Alone, we cannot face "the mystery of iniquity" with impunity. Only Christ can overcome the powers of evil. Only in and through Him can we survive...

Let's take a closer look at our weapons for battling darkness:

> 1. Truth (Belt of Truth) - The only way to know the difference between the good guys and the bad guys is to measure them by the truth exemplified in Jesus and explained in the Bible.

Truth breeds integrity. With truth fastened to us, we have integrity which Satan as the father of lies cannot withstand.

2. Righteousness (Breastplate of Righteousness) - If we hang out with God, God will hang out with us. It's a simple equation: holiness = happiness (see Secret 10). That's why Max Lucado wrote in *Walking with the Savior* (1993), "Run to Jesus. Jesus wants you to go to Him. He wants to become the most important person in your life, the greatest love you'll ever know. He wants you to go to Him. He wants you to love Him so much that there's no room in your heart and in your life for sin." And note this well! No matter how good we are or become, we're never good enough to save ourselves. We're *never* righteous enough to save ourselves. As Martyn Lloyd-Jones confirmed in *The Christian Soldier* (1977), "Not hell, nor anything else can penetrate the righteousness of Jesus Christ...So whatever the assault may be...we know that we are quite secure and that finally nothing can separate us from the love of God which is in Christ Jesus our Lord."

3. Discipline (Battle Boots) – *The New International Version* translation is clear: "Feet fitted with the gospel of peace as a firm footing." *The English Standard Version* highlights "the *readiness* given by the gospel of peace." A solid foundation begins with faith in Jesus (see Matthew 7:24-27) and grows through spiritual disciplines: worship, prayer, Bible study, fasting, sacrament, silence, stewardship, and fellowship with believers.

4. Faith (Shield of Faith) – Faith repels "the flaming darts" or assaults of darkness. When we are *in the Spirit* through spiritual disciplines, those *out of the Spirit* cannot penetrate our minds, hearts, and souls. Complete trust in God is our greatest protection. Or as the psalmist sang in the inspiration of Luther's great battle hymn "A Mighty Fortress Is Our God," "God is our refuge and strength, an ever-present help in trouble. Therefore we will not fear..." (Psalm 46).

5. Christmindedness (Helmet of Salvation) – Simply, keep focused on Jesus! If Jesus is in our heads and hearts, we're *headed* in the right direction. Psalm 91:14-16 proclaims the

promise, "Because he loves me, says the Lord, I will rescue him; I will protect him, for he acknowledges my name. He will call upon me, and I will answer him; I will be with him in trouble, I will deliver him and honor him. With long life will I satisfy him and show him my salvation." Certainty of personal salvation and confirmation of that salvation through the "signs of salvation" in our confession, conduct, countenance, and conscience throttle Satan.

6. Bible (Sword of the Spirit) – The Bible is God's revealed rule for discipleship. Or as Peter explained, "Above all, you must understand that no prophecy of Scripture came about by the prophet's own interpretation. For prophecy never had its origin in the will of man, but men spoke from God as they were carried along by the Holy Spirit" (2 Peter 1:20-21). Paul concluded without equivocation, "All Scripture is *God-breathed*" (2 Timothy 3:16). That's why we *attend to* rather than *contend with* the Bible. We don't read the Bible and say, "Well, I think..." We announce, "Thus saith the Lord." Rather than debating the content, we pray and labor to enflesh the content in our lives. The Westminster Divines were emphatic in Question 2 of *The Shorter Catechism* (1646), "The Word of God which is contained in the Scriptures of the Old and New Testaments is the only rule to direct us how we may glorify and enjoy Him." Dr. Lloyd-Jones echoed, "You must gird yourselves with...truth. If you do not, you are defeated. And I am asserting...truth can be known, that there is an authority. It is not reason...feeling...any church. It is the Book called the Bible."

7. Prayer - *The Living Bible*: "Pray all the time. Ask God for anything in line with the Holy Spirit's wishes. Plead with Him, reminding Him of your needs, and keep praying earnestly for all Christians everywhere. Pray for me, too, and ask God to give me the right words as I boldly tell others about the Lord." Somebody said, "To clasp the hands in prayer is the beginning of an uprising against the disorder of the world." William Barclay wrote *(Ephesians,* 1956), "Finally, Paul comes to the greatest weapon of all – and that

is prayer. We note three things that he says about prayer...It must be constant...It must be intense...It must be unselfish."

A few things should be in mind as we put on God's armor:

1. Our strength is in the Lord. "In conclusion," Dr. Phillips paraphrased, "be strong - not in yourselves but in the Lord, in the power of His boundless strength." *The Message* urges, "Be prepared. You're up against far more than you can handle on your own. Take all the help you can get, every weapon God has issued, so that when it's all over but the shouting you'll still be on your feet." F.F. Bruce commented in *The Epistle to the Ephesians* (1961), "For wrestling or fighting on the human plane, human strength will suffice. But it is not on the human plane that the Christian warfare is fought out, but in the spiritual realm, and in that realm only spiritual resources can avail. In himself the Christian is incapable of gaining the mastery over the principalities and powers that would fain bring him into bondage: only the power of Christ can help him." Fortunately, as Luther taught us to sing, "Did we in our own strength confide, our striving would be losing...The prince of darkness grim, we tremble not for him...His rage we can endure, for lo, his doom is sure, one little word shall fell him." Jesus!

2. Wearing all of the battle gear is required for victory. *A little-dab'll-do-ya* isn't enough. We must put on *the whole armor.* Dr. Lloyd-Jones wrote, "As the enemy is still waiting, and watching in his subtlety, ingenuity and power, there is only one way to stand...Take unto you the whole armor which God has provided for you...Leave no unguarded place in your soul."

3. If Satan is up to no good in your life, you must be doing

something right! John Eldredge observed in *Wild at Heart* (2001), "Do you know why there's been such an assault? The Enemy fears you. You are dangerous big-time. If you ever really got your heart back, lived from it with courage, you would be a huge problem to him. You would do a lot of damage...on the side of good." Satan does not waste energies on Christians and churches that aren't doing anything *for God's sake.* But when Christians and churches are honoring God, helping people, and advancing the Kingdom in the name of Jesus, Satan will attack. That's when we must take the battle to him; already knowing, of course, we're going to win!

If you're being oppressed by evil forces, here's your victory prayer:

Father, I thank You for providing all I need to overcome the attacks of darkness in my life and to live triumphantly amid the meanness, madness, and misery of life in the modern world. With the assist of Your Holy Spirit, I put on the battle gear to defeat the enemy:

The Belt of Truth - Your will as exemplified in Jesus and explained in the Bible.

The Breastplate of Righteousness - The *covering* of Christ's blood and righteousness which makes up for my sins even as I pray and labor to live a holy life to honor You, help people, and advance the Kingdom *on earth as it is in heaven.*

Gospel Shoes - The firm foundation of faith in Jesus as Lord and Savior; cultivating my personal relationship with Him through worship, prayer, Bible study, fasting, sacrament, silence, stewardship, and fellowship with believers.

The Shield of Faith - I trust Your existential and eternal

care with the psalmist, "I have been young, and now am old, yet I have not seen the righteous forsaken" (Psalm 37:25).

The Helmet of Salvation - With Jesus as my Lord and Savior, I know where I'm headed *in the end* and how to live *in the meantime.*

The Sword of the Spirit - Your Holy Bible is "a lamp to my feet and a light to my path" (Psalm 119:105).

Prayer - Communion with You is the pulse of my life. Begging your assistance in putting on Your armor *and keeping it on,* I want to be a salt-shaker and light-bearer for Christ's sake; preserving the good, purifying the bad, and bringing joy into all relationships as I shine for Him in all things at all times.

Again, thank You, Lord, for providing weapons to defeat darkness; reserving my highest praise and thanks for Jesus whose name alone exorcises anyone and anything allied with the evil one.

I pray as I seek to live in the name of Jesus. Amen.

Let me reiterate our greatest defense *and offense* against darkness in one *Word.*

Jesus!!!

Repeating His promise, "I will build my church, and the gates of hell shall not prevail against it."

Paraphrasing a bit, "I will save my people, and the power behind darkness and death will not overpower them."

It's like a friend who says, "I've been reading the Bible and I've peeked to see how it ends. *Jesus wins!!!*"

Zeb Bradford Long rejoiced in *Passage through the Wilderness* (1998), "The first rule in spiritual warfare...is to be firmly grounded in Jesus Christ, because outside of Him we are vulnerable and powerless. He alone is enough; we need nothing beyond Him."

I really like the way Francis Frangipane asserted this good news in *The Three Battlegrounds* (1989), "How do we defeat the enemy? Victory begins with the name of Jesus on our lips; it is consummated by the nature of Jesus in our hearts."

We sing with Luther, "The prince of darkness grim, we tremble not for him...One little word shall fell him...Dost ask who that may be? Christ Jesus, it is He!"

It's Secret 8: "While never underestimating *poneros,* never doubt Jesus as *kurios* of all."

A friend quipped, "When Satan comes knocking at your door, all you have to do is say, 'Jesus, please get that for me.' "

Victory is assured, therefore, the moment after opening the door to Jesus: "Behold, I stand at the door and knock. If anyone hears my voice and opens the door, I will come in to him and eat with him and he with me" (Revelation 3:20).

So if you have never invited Jesus into your heart as Lord and Savior, or if you need to renew your saving relationship with Him, please pray with me right now:

Lord, I trust You as Father-Creator, Saving Son Jesus, and sustaining Holy Spirit. I know You love me not because of who I am and what I do but in spite of who I am and what I do. You proved that love for all time in the birth, life, crucifixion, and resurrection of Jesus. I am sorry for my sins - the ways that I have rejected Your will for my life. I need Your love, forgiveness, and mercy. I welcome You into my heart, mind, soul, and body as Lord. I thank You for guaranteeing my eternal life and enabling my confident

131

living. I ask Your Holy Spirited help to honor You in all things at all times by loving like Jesus as I pray in His name. Amen.

SECRET 9

We are not responsible for the beliefs and behaviors of others; but we are responsible for our response.

Christians believe in divine predestination; or God's guiding from *before* womb to *after* tomb.

Paul explained (Romans 8:28-30),

> **And we know that for those who love God all things work together for good, for those who are called according to His purpose. For those whom He foreknew He also predestined to be conformed to the image of His Son, in order that He might be the firstborn among many brothers. And those whom He called He also justified, and those whom He justified He also glorified...**

The apostle echoed the prophet: "Before I formed you in the womb I knew you, and before you were born I consecrated you" (Jeremiah 1:5).

Or as the Westminster Divines asserted in *The Shorter Catechism* of 1646 (Question 7), "The decrees of God are His eternal purpose, according to the counsel of His will, whereby, for His own glory, *He hath foreordained whatsoever comes to pass.*"

Realistically, the paradox of Biblical affirmations of divine predestination and human volition (e.g., Joshua 24:15; Revelation 3:20) is too *divine* for *human* comprehension. God *being God* is beyond the grasp of existential definition and full discernment. The horizontal

133

is not positioned to attain complete knowledge of the vertical. Or as Luther often quipped, "Let God *be* God!"

I recall a story from seminary about a professor lecturing on this paradox. He asked, "How do we reconcile predestation and free will?" Moving to a student who was dozing off, he slammed his hand on the desk and shouted, "What's the answer?" The seminarian shot up and said, "I knew yesterday but forgot." The professor shook his head and lamented, "What a pity! The only man who knew *and he forgot!"*

Even John Calvin who is awarded credit for the finest articulation of double predestination – God's foreordination of who is going to heaven and hell – accepted rather than debated this paradox. While deferring to God's determination of all things with all people at all times in assent to His omniscience by virtue of His omnipotence, even hyper-Calvinists who, unlike Calvin, are more *Calvinistic* than Biblical must admit his commentaries, sermons, and *Institutes of the Christian Religion* focus far more on volition in discipleship than some kind of puppet-by-the-strings predestination.

Indeed, one could preach a sermon titled "Predestined, But Free to Choose" as an exercise as well as expression of Biblical fidelity.

Parenthetically, I've often said the person who figures out this paradox apart from accepting God's ways being beyond our intellectual attainment will be the next guest on Oprah.

Paul was right: *"Now* we see in a mirror dimly, but *then* face to face. *Now* I know in part; *then* I shall know fully" (1 Corinthians 13:12).

Recognizing *human* inability to alter *divine* predestination, it seems far more prudent to concentrate on praying and laboring to make the right choices in consonance with Biblical and Christological revelation than to fret over a predestination beyond interference; unless, of course, you need something to fill up time in a church's adult forum or Philosophy 101.

Why waste so much energy and emotion on a paradox beyond intellectual and spiritual discernment in this time and space? It makes more sense to "trust and obey, for there's no other way to be happy in Jesus, but to trust and obey."

Or as some say, "Do your best, and let God do the rest...Let go and let God."

Nevertheless, Christians affirm and always eventually appreciate God's guiding in their lives.

Christians know nothing happens by accident in their lives.

Life is *designed* by divine intentions.

Our Lord guides us into *certain* circumstances at *certain* times with *certain* people to work His will in, through, and for us.

Again, that's what we understand as God's predestination; or His *directing us* to be where and when with whom so we can honor Him in obedience to His expressed will in Jesus and the Bible.

These situations and experiences are *divine appointments*. God has a reason for placing us in time and space.

God expects us to be messengers and ambassadors of His Gospel.

I think of a call from a very angry woman about a sermon that I had preached on the radio.

She started right in, "That was one of the worst sermons

135

I've ever heard. You have no idea what you're talking about."

It doesn't take very long for pastors to get used to being paid to be abused as well as holy. I remember my first session meeting as moderator – that's *Presbyterian* for *pastor* – when an elder asked after I outlined my ideas for church growth, "Are you out of your mind? We're not doing any of that! You're crazy!" Not long after that, I started telling prospective pastors, "If you'd like to know what it's like to be a pastor, put on a deerskin and go walking through the woods on the first day of hunting season."

Be that as it is, I've never lived for such criticism. She brought to mind the lamb who said to the lion, "O.K., but you lie down first." And when I found out she wasn't even a member of the church anyway, I had to bite my lip and recite 1 Corinthians 13 under my breath.

I said, "I hear you saying you didn't like my sermon."

She screamed, "Are you deaf or something? I didn't say I didn't like your sermon! I said it was awful! It was one of the worst sermons that I've ever heard in my life! You don't know what the hell you're talking about!"

Ding! Ding! Ding!

End of round one.

I came out smoking for round two.

I've always felt a sermon not worth preaching twice isn't worth preaching once. If she didn't like it the first time, I'd see how she liked the replay.

The sermon in dispute was on the parable of the prodigal son (Luke 15:11-32).

So I began to review the sermon line by line.

She kept trying to interrupt; saying the older son was the real hero of the story, the younger son should have

136

been disowned, the older son was noble and loyal, the younger son was irresponsible and should have been turned away when he returned home, the father was too tolerant and forgiving, and just about everything contrary to accepted interpretations of the parable.

Around ten minutes into the bout, it hit me.

I was talking to the older brother of the parable!

"Excuse me," I inquired much less combatively with renewed pastoral concern, "but do you have a younger brother or sister who hurt you?"

She began to sob.

It was a divine appointment.

We didn't spend any more time on the parable. We talked about love and grace and forgiveness. We talked about Jesus.

In my selfishness and defensiveness and need to be right at the expense of loving, I almost missed an opportunity to share the redemptive possibilities for her family through Jesus.

Jerry Kirk, former pastor of Cincinnati's College Hill Presbyterian Church and founder of the National Coalition Against Pornography, shared his divine appointment to battle pornography with me back in the 80s.

Seeing the devastating effects of pornography on several families in the church, Jerry went to the top of a hill and shouted, "God, why don't *You* do something?" God shouted back, "Jerry, why don't *you* do something?"

That was Jerry's call to take on the evil of pornography; and he didn't wait for somebody else to do what our Lord had called him to do. He didn't waste energy and emotion responding to what others were or were not doing to promote righteousness or right behavior as profiled in

Jesus and prescribed in the Bible. He prayed and labored for righteousness. He accepted *His* divine appointment.

It's Secret 9: "We are not responsible for the beliefs and behaviors of others; but we are responsible for our response."

Christians don't wait around for others to do what God has called them to do.

Instead of complaining about the way things are, Christians press forward to how things ought to be.

Christians look up, stand up, speak up, and act up for Jesus! Christians are proactive not reactive; actively promoting righteousness in the world, church, and themselves. "There is only one corner of the universe you can be certain of improving," Aldous Huxley said, "and that's your own self."

Someone said sarcastically, "The problem in this world is too many people think of changing everybody but themselves."

Jesus put it this way (Matthew 7:3-5),

Why do you see the speck that is in your brother's eye, but do not notice the log that is in your eye? Or how can you say to your brother, 'Let me take the speck out of your eye,' when there is the log in your own eye? You hypocrite, first take the log out of your own eye, and then you will see clearly to take the speck out of your brother's eye.

You may have heard about the dying fellow who said to his wife, "My dear, you have been with me through all the bad times. When I got fired, you were there. When my business failed, you were there. When we lost the house, you were there. When my health failed, you were there." After a pause, he continued, "I think you've been bad luck."

Then there was the guy who was whacked on the head with a frying pan by his wife while reading the newspaper. "Why did you do that?" he yelled. She yelled back, "That was for the piece of paper in your pants with the name Eloise on it!" "No, no, no," he protested, "I bet on a horse named Eloise at the races last night." "Please forgive me," his wife begged, "because I should have trusted you." A few days later, he was whacked on the head again with that same frying pan; and he was hit so hard that he was knocked out cold. When he regained consciousness, he asked, "Why did you do that?" She snarled, "Your horse called."

If you're like me, perpetual victims are especially pathetic. You know the kind.

They're always throwing self-pity parties because everybody's against them and nothing ever goes their way and nobody likes them or appreciates them and it's always somebody else's fault and so on.

Blah. Blah. Blah.

Wah. Wah. Wah.

My friend Jim Tuckett wrote about "Taking Responsibility Versus Being a Victim" to his e-mail subscribers on 26 January 2003:

Let's see if I understand how it works lately...

> If a woman burns her thighs on the hot coffee she was holding in her lap while driving, she blames the restaurant.
>
> If your teen-age son kills himself, you blame the rock 'n roll music or musicians he liked.
>
> If you smoke three packs a day for 40 years and die of lung cancer, your family blames the tobacco company.
>
> If your daughter gets pregnant by the football captain, you blame the school for poor sex education.

If your neighbor crashes into a tree while driving home drunk, you blame the bartender.

If your cousin gets AIDS because the needle he used to shoot up with heroin was dirty, you blame the government for not providing clean ones.

If your grandchildren are rude brats without manners, you blame television.

If your friend is shot by a deranged madman, you blame the gun manufacturer.

And if a crazed person breaks into the cockpit and tries to kill the pilots at 35,000 feet, and the passengers kill him instead, the mother of the deceased blames the airline.

I think people who are always making personal excuses or blaming others for their failures, miscues, misfortune, and bad behaviors need to be strapped to an uncomfortable chair and forced to listen to "Get Over It" by Don Henley and Glenn Frey (The Eagles):

> I turn on the tube and what do I see
> A whole lotta people cryin' "Don't blame me"
> They point their crooked little fingers at everybody else
> Spend all their time feelin' sorry for themselves
> Victim of this, victim of that
> Your momma's too thin; your daddy's too fat
>
> Get over it
> Get over it
> All this whinin' and cryin' and pitchin' a fit
> Get over it
> Get over it

When we're crying out to God for Him to do something like Dr. Kirk on that hill in Cincinnati so long ago, our Lord is blasting back, "Why don't *you* do something?"

Here's what we're supposed to do: "The only thing that

counts is faith expressing itself through love" (Galatians 5:6).

That's the standard operating procedure for Christians.

That's our *modus operandi.*

That's our *raison d'etre.*

That's our *beruf.*

Whatever you want to call it, *the proof of the pudding for Christians is faith expressed through love.*

Instead of bantering and moaning about what others are doing and how they're behaving, our faith and ethic hold us responsible for how we respond to life's opportunities, challenges, ups, downs, detours, distractions, joys, sorrows, victories, defeats, and all the rest.

Instead of fretting, we're supposed to be faithful.

It's Secret 9.

And Galatians 5:6 is the meat for those bones.

Let's take a closer look,

First, the apostle refuted the efficacy of superficial acts of righteousness: "For in Christ Jesus neither circumcision nor uncircumcision has any value" (5:6a).

He did not say rites like circumcision, baptism, and the like are not important; but he insisted their importance is linked to behaviors confirming symbolic rituals and ceremonies.

It's like the folks who want to get little Johnny or Susie *done;* which is the unchurched's way of requesting baptism. I confess I've always wanted to ask, "And how do you want your child *done?* Rare? Medium? Well done?"

God knows some folks just go through the motions.

I recall the trustee who complained to the pastor about

bats in the church. The pastor said, "No problem. I'll just baptize 'em and we'll never see 'em again."

Trinkets and tipping instead of tithing and *simple-Simon-says* religiosity along with C&E Christianity (i.e., folks showing up twice a year at *Christmas and Easter* to wink at God in worship) are bastardized Christianity.

Too many circumcised, baptized, cross-wearing, bumper-sticker-bearing, church-membership-roll-appearing "Christians" don't do much good *for Christ's sake*.

An awful illustration of such hypocrisy or *wearing the mask of Christianity while incarnating antithetical behaviors* comes from my favorite seminary.

Some students and professors at the neighboring university decided to test the integrity of the seminarians. They concocted a *preaching contest* in the chapel on the parable of the good Samaritan (Luke 10:25-37).

They hired an actor who would pretend to be drunk and passed out on the steps leading into the chapel. In order to get into the chapel to preach a sermon on the parable of the good Samaritan, the seminarians would have to cross paths with someone in need.

Obviously, the test was to see if the aspiring pastors and ambassadors of good will would *practice* what they were about to *preach.*

Sadly, not one seminarian stopped to provide assistance on their way into the chapel to preach a sermon on our Lord's story of how Christianity is enfleshed in selfless service and care for the desperate.

While our Lord used the poetry of a parable to highlight this dimension of discipleship, the apostle was precisely propositional: The only thing that counts is *faith expressing itself through love."*

Faith (πιστις - *pistis*) is not some two-feet-planted-firmly-in-the-air feeling. It is a conviction, certainty, and confidence in God evoked by education about and experiences of Father, Son, and Holy Spirit.

Faith *expresses* (ενεργεω - *energeo*) itself or shows its "true colors" *through* (δια - *dia*) or by means of *love*.

The Greeks used language with precision; and they had four different words for love. Understanding the differences enables us to recognize the particular responsibilities of Christianity's distinctive love ethic (viz., αγαπη - *agape*) :

1. **ερως** *(eros)* - While not appearing in the New Testament, this is romantic love. It is the kind of passionate affection expressed within the context of marital fidelity in the Song of Solomon. C.S. Lewis defined this love in *The Four Loves* (1960): "By eros I mean...that state which we call 'being in love'; or, if you prefer, that kind of love which lovers are 'in.' " It can have a narcotic effect; blinding reality to the bliss, mist, and dog-eyed stares of the relationship. Though a blessing in its proper marital context, it can be destructive extra-maritally; as in the old adage not bound to age, "Puppy love can lead to a dog's life."

2. **στοργη** *(storge)* - This is family-affection-blood-is-thicker-than-water love. Especially noticed in parent-child relationships, it does not appear in the New Testament apart from compounded forms in Romans 1:31, 12:10, and 2 Timothy 3:3.

3. **φιλεω** *(phileo)* - *Philadelphia* (brotherly love) comes to mind. "A friend will, to be sure," detailed Lewis, "prove himself to be also an ally when alliance becomes necessary; will lend or give when we are in need, nurse us in sickness, stand up for us among our enemies, do what he can for our widows and orphans." This is the love of common insight and interest. It is the deep bond reserved for those who are *near and dear* to us.

4. αγαπη *(agape)* - As an attitude rather than affection generated less by emotions than intellectual volition and spiritual devotion, this love *expresses itself* by praying and working for the highest good for others regardless of who, what, where, or when without the need or expectation for response, regard, or reward.

Christianity is distinguished by its αγαπη *(agape)* love ethic; declaring allegiance to and affection for God through charitable creeds and deeds for all of God's children without discrimination. This love functions at the command of Matthew 25: "As you do it for them, you do it for me."

"Therefore," wrote John Calvin, "is charity an infallible sign and token that we be willing to serve God."

Tony Campolo has often shared an experience in Hawaii during a preaching mission which illustrated Christian love in action.

He arrived very late on the night before he was scheduled to preach. He was hungry. The only place which was open was one of those greasy spoons where bugs scurry around when you pick up the menu from the slick table.

As Tony was eating, a bunch of hookers walked in. They went to the counter and one announced, "Tomorrow's my birthday!" Another snapped, "So why you tellin' us?" Sheepishly, the reply came, "I don't know. I just thought you might like to know."

After they left, Tony asked the waitress if they came in around the same time every night. When the waitress said they did, Tony said, "Let's have a birthday party for her tomorrow night." "O.K.," the cook chimed in, "I'll bake the cake."

144

Tony arrived a little early the next night and decorated the diner with balloons and streamers.

When the hookers showed up, they had a birthday party.

"Cut the cake!" someone yelled.

But the birthday girl couldn't do it. Slowly and quietly, she said, "I've never had a birthday cake. Do you mind if I just take it home and put it in the freezer?" Then she left with the cake.

After she left, Tony asked everyone to pray with him.

Tony sat in the diner with the waitress and cook after the birthday party in deafening silence.

Finally, the cook looked at Tony and said, "I didn't know you were a preacher. What kind of church do you belong to?"

Tony announced, "I belong to the kind of church that throws birthday parties for hookers at two in the morning."

The cook paused a moment and then said, "I could join that kind of church."

I got into some trouble as a young pastor for starting a sermon like this:

How many prostitutes do we have with us this morning? How about parolees and ex-convicts? Anybody here who has cheated on your spouse lately? How about recovering substance abusers?

Can I see your hands? Where are the hands?

Are you telling me that we've only got pure and perfect people in attendance today?

While God knows that isn't true, if anybody, and I mean anybody, doesn't feel welcomed, included, and loved in our worship services, then it's time for us to get down on our knees, confess our sins of exclusion and pride, beg forgiveness, and then get off of our knees and start inviting people into this building until it starts looking like a church.

Take a long look at your church.

Jesus said, "Come to me, **all** who labor and are heavy laden, and I will give you rest" (Matthew 11:28).

Paul said, "You are **all** one in Christ Jesus" (Galatians 3:28).

If your church does not include *all of the below,* it's time for *you* to invite *them.*

Don't wait for somebody else to do what God expects you to do! It's Secret 9.

It's the command that commends or condemns, "As you do it for them, you do it for me."

SECRET 10

Holiness = Happiness
(i.e., the holier we are, the happier we are!)

There's a miracle happening in Rockford, Illinois.

Women and men who love Jesus are crossing color, class, culture, and denominational distinctions for worship at least once a month as Greater Rockford in Prayer and Praise (GRIPP).

Building upon a February 1995 vision entrusted to Dr. Bob Griffin, President of Rockford Renewal Ministries, that the appointed moment (καιρος - *kairos)* has arrived for God's people to shed human fetters of racial, religious, and socioeconomic separations and come together for worship, service, and evangelism, GRIPP is hosted by churches committed to the Biblical call to unity (e.g., 2 Chronicles 7:14; John 17:20-23):

> **If my people who are called by my name humble themselves, and pray and seek my face and turn from their wicked ways, then I will hear from heaven and will forgive their sin and heal their land...**
>
> **I do not ask for these only, but also for those who will believe in me through their word, that they may all be one, just as you, Father, are in me, and I in you, that they also may be in us, so that the world may believe that you have sent me. The glory that you have given me I have given to them, that they may be one even as we are one, I in them and you in me, that they may become perfectly one, so that the world may know that you sent me and loved them**

even as you loved me.

Actually, GRIPP has evolved from *concerts of prayer* which began in 1995 and culminated at the 25th City-Wide Concert of Prayer in Rockford's Coronado Theatre on 4 October 2002.

That last concert at the Coronado will be remembered as a bold step into the future as Dr. Griffin announced, "People of other faiths might not appreciate this, but we have this idea of crowning Jesus as King over Rockford at the place of coronation – the Coronado."

Predictably, a few non-Christians who think Christians will abandon their confession at the drop of a politically correct hat were offended by Dr. Griffin's authentic Christianity. They even wrote letters to local newspapers to declare their outrage. Amid the heat generated by light, I told Bob, "It's too bad we've reached that point in which assisting positive pluralism in the community means masking our individualities. Only when we have the integrity to say what we believe, can we establish the kind of trust that will enable the pursuit of common goals."

Surprisingly, "Christians" joined the assault. One said he was "disappointed, appalled, frustrated, and shocked." Another chirped about "triumphalist Christian ideology." Dr. Griffin exposed their lukewarm religion to outright apostasy in a simple assessment: "The Bible itself says that the Bible is offensive to those that don't believe. I'm happy to take criticism for the truth which I embrace."

The war of words through local newspapers and clergy conclaves proved my conclusion about unconverted clergy who don't really believe in Jesus as attested by the New Testament yet are duplicitously hypocritical enough to pick up checks from churches that have traditionally, historically, confessionally, and constitutionally acknowledged the unique saving Lordship (King*ship*) of Jesus Christ (see page 84).

The irony of those criticizing this rapidly growing unity overcoming diversity through common and unmasked faith in Jesus is the critics and cynics represent religions, institutions, and organizations advocating *but not demonstrating* the joys of indiscriminate community so apparent at every gathering of GRIPP.

The growth of GRIPP *in the face of* rabid rebukes from *very white* socioeconomic and ecclesiastical elites testifies to the accelerating decline of mainline religion in America. While the familiar mainline denominations are old homogeneous wineskins cracking at the seams and losing members quicker than Michael Jackson's Fan Club, GRIPP is Rockford's expression of a spiritual movement sweeping people up into unity disrespecting previous exclusions.

Rockford's Christian community gathering with increasing regularity as GRIPP has not paid much attention to the naysayers; regarding them as irrelevant to the advancement of Jesus Christ's Kingdom *on earth as it is in heaven.* Or as Edward Sharp wrote in a letter to the editor of the *Rockford Register Star* on 2 December 2002,

> Again, I say this issue that has been voiced by Bob Griffin is a nonissue. Jesus the Christ is already the Lord of Rockford, the United States, and the world! There are those that do not recognize the truth but will some day.

I've been saying for almost two decades that the lampstand or *efficacious place in the Kingdom* is being transferred to those who are seizing the appointed moment (καιρος - *kairos)* and moving with God as profiled in Jesus and prescribed in the Bible (see Revelation 2:1-7).

While sociologists of religion and membership statistics have substantiated my suspicion for several years, GRIPP has provided the clearest and most conclusive apocalypse of this transfer for me. I see a joy, wholeness, happiness, evangelistic fervor, sacrificial attitude of service, existential unity, and eternal security unknown to contemporary mainline denominations which are breaking down all of the old ecclesiastical, color, class, and culture boundaries.

The good news of Rockford's miracle is spreading across America; but you won't hear much about it from local mainliners who aren't involved or media who are more interested in heralding the irenic potential of Islam.

It doesn't really matter.

An old camp song comes to mind:

> It only takes a spark to get a fire going.
> And soon all those around can warm up in its glowing. That's how it is with God's love,
> Once you've experienced it,
> You spread His love to everyone;
> You want to pass it on.
>
> What a wondrous time is spring, when all the trees are budding;
> The birds begin to sing, the flowers start their blooming. That's how it is with God's love;
> Once you've experienced it,
> You want to sing
> "It's fresh like spring":
> You want to pass it on.
>
> I wish for you my friend, this happiness that I've found.
> You can depend on Him,
> It matters not where you're bound.
> I'll shout it from the mountain top,

I want the world to know;
The Lord of love has come to me,
I want to pass it on.

The good news is being written all over the faces and actions of the faithful.

GRIPP is a powerful witness to Secret 10: "Holiness = Happiness (i.e., the holier we are, the happier we are!)."

Holiness is a state of heart, mind, and soul.

Holiness or *sanctification* or *consecration* is a process beginning at conversion to Christ and continuing until we meet Him face to face after the last breath; praying and laboring to be different from the world as increasingly transformed by the Word in Jesus and the Bible.

Embracing and emulating holiness do not provide an escape from the world, but it does provoke a passionate determination to be *in* but *not* of the world:

- Necessity prevails over materialism.

- Food provides physical fuel and personal pleasure but does not feed gluttony.

- Sleep restores the body but is not an excuse for laziness.

- Sex is celebrated in but not apart from marriage.

- Money is a tool to serve God not selfishness.

- Position, prestige, and power are instruments for advancing the Kingdom rather than personal desire.

- Work and play balance but don't dominate each other.

Holiness is separating ourselves from the ways of the world by devotion to God's will as exemplified in Jesus and explained in the Bible.

Particularly, holiness is nurtured through spiritual disciplines: worship, prayer, Bible study, fasting, sacrament, silence, stewardship, and fellowship with believers.

The payoff of holiness is happiness.

Or as Jesus promised in detailing some of the character traits of believers (Matthew 5:1-12),

> **Happy are the poor in spirit, for theirs is the kingdom of heaven.**
>
> **Happy are those who mourn, for they shall be comforted.**
>
> **Happy are the meek, for they shall inherit the earth.**
>
> **Happy are those who hunger and thirst for righteousness, for they shall be satisfied.**
>
> **Happy are the merciful, for they shall receive mercy.**
>
> **Happy are the pure in heart, for they shall see God.**
>
> **Happy are the peacemakers, for they shall be called *sons of God*.**
>
> **Happy are those who are persecuted for righteousness' sake, for theirs is the kingdom of heaven.**
>
> **Happy are you when others revile you and persecute you and utter all kinds of evil against you falsely on my account. Rejoice and be glad, for your reward is great in heaven, for so they persecuted the prophets who were before you.**

Proverbs 3:5-10 sums up the attitude of holiness (dedication to God) which leads to holy acts (deeds for God):

> **Trust in the Lord with all your heart, and do not lean on your own understanding. In all your ways**

acknowledge Him, and He will make straight your paths. Be not wise in your own eyes; fear the Lord, and turn away from evil. It will be healing to your flesh and refreshment to your bones. Honor the Lord with your wealth and with the firstfruits of all your produce; then your barns will be filled with plenty...

I think of holiness as *choosing to be on God's side.*

Holiness is leaving the world's side on issues of faith and morality and allying with Jesus and the Bible in all things at all times with all people.

Holiness is saying with Joshua, "Choose this day whom you will serve...But as for me and my house, we will serve the Lord" (see Joshua 24).

It takes spine to be holy!

Holiness is the devoted determination to be God's without reference to the cost.

Harking back to Secret 1, it's like the pastor who had just been called to a church. He was asked, "How do you expect to please so many people?" He answered, "I did not come here to please *so many people.* I came here to please *One!*"

Martin Niemoller comes to mind.

He was a German Lutheran pastor who helped organize the Confessing Church of Germany which opposed Adolf Hitler. He was arrested by the Gestapo on 1 July 1937 and imprisoned at Sachsenhausen and then Dachau. Reflecting on what happens when holiness is compromised by worldliness, he said,

> In Germany they came first for the Communists, and I didn't speak up because I wasn't a Communist.
> Then they came for the Jews, and I didn't speak up because I wasn't a Jew.

Then they came for the trade unionists, and I didn't speak up because I wasn't a trade unionist.

Then they came for the Catholics, and I didn't speak up because I was a Protestant.

Then they came for me, and by that time no one was left to speak up.

How vital it is for us to keep in mind our distinctive love ethic (αγαπη - *agape)*. Just as God loves the world (see John 3:16-17), we are called to love it too; praying and laboring for the existential and eternal best for all of the below by command of all of the above.

In my many visits to Dachau as a student in the early 70s and then later as a tourist and tour guide, I often thought of Pastor Niemoller's witness.

Regardless of the weather, I have always been *chilled* at Dachau. It remains one of the most grotesque examples of inhumanity and unholiness. 160,000 slave laborers were confined in that one concentration camp under subhuman conditions before liberation. Aside from the Satanically inspired facilities for mass murder and cremation with meat hooks used to warehouse the bodies of our Lord's children, Dachau was the site of brutally unspeakable medical experiments – that's a euphemism for Nazi butchering – on over 3500 prisoners. God only knows how many of God's children were slaughtered by those German demons at Dachau.

Despite knowing more than 6 million people (mostly Jews) perished in those houses of hell and not forgetting that millions more were exterminated outside of the camps, the horror is still unimaginable to people in countries like America which have been insulated from such barbarity by relatively civilized borders.

That's why I scolded a retired pastor who served un-

154

der Hitler after he came to see me and complained about theologians like me who continue to refer to Germany's national sins surrounding World War II, "I pray to God that we'll never stop because God forbid that it should happen again."

When we don't learn from history's pejoratives, they repeat themselves.

God knows we haven't learned from history.

Having witnessed the reincarnations of Nazism and anti-Semitism in Austria, France, and Germany myself beginning in the early 70s and continuing into the 21st century, I was not surprised by their exposed complicity in the evils of Iraq under Hussein along with their damning silence about Islam's hate homiletics.

That's why I carry two stones from Dachau in my pocket. I picked them up during my last visit in 2000.

One is white to remind me of the purity of holiness which honors God by helping all of God's children

One is red to remind me of the floods of blood that have been spilled because of unholy alliances.

I carry them as my burden; praying God's help not to add to His and *His*.

A few anonymous lines crossed my desk recently:

I had a *drug* problem when I was a young person. I was *drug* to church on Sunday morning. I was *drug* to church on Sunday night. I was *drug* to church on Wednesday night. I was *drug* to Sunday School. I was *drug* to Vacation Bible School. I was *drug* to Confirmation Class. I was *drug* to youth group. I was *drug* to pray with my family. I was also *drug* to the woodshed when I disobeyed my parents, told a lie, brought home a bad report card, or did not speak with respect.

155

Those *drugs* are still in my veins; and they affect my behavior in nearly everything I think, say, and do. They are stronger than cocaine, crack, and heroin.

If more children had this *drug* problem, America would be a better place.

It's Secret 10.

I don't know anybody who gets into trouble by being holy.

I don't know anybody who gets into trouble in worship, prayer, Bible study, fasting, sacrament, silence, stewardship, and fellowship with authentic Christians.

Holiness is being so increasingly filled with Jesus that there's less and less and less space for the kind of stuff that breeds bad behavior.

It's like the fellow who approached a mystical hot dog vendor and said, "I'll take one of everything." After giving a twenty dollar bill to the vendor, he asked, "Where's my change?" And the mystic answered, "All change must come from within."

You may have heard of the man in search of a Christian pet. Finally, he bought a parrot because the pet store owner said the bird had never uttered a foul word. But after forgetting to feed the parrot before going to work one day, it cursed a blue streak when the man returned. So the man put the bird in the freezer for a minute and then said, "If you ever swear like that again, I'm going to put you back in the freezer for five minutes." "O.K., O.K.," the shivering parrot said, "but I have one question. What did that turkey in there say?"

I'm reminded of the woman who said she felt like saying "Amen" and "Praise the Lord" during worship every now and then; but she was concerned about what people would think of her. I said, "That's your problem."

We can never be holy and we can never be happy as long as we're more concerned about what people think of us than what honors God. Again, it's all about choosing sides.

Holiness is all about placing God first in our lives.

Happiness is the payoff.

Augustine put it this way: "You are great, O Lord, and greatly to be praised...You have made us for yourself, and our hearts are restless until they rest in You" *(The Confessions,* 397-400).

If we're searching for happiness in this life, we don't really need to stock up on all of those self-help books. We can save a lot of money by following the simple formula of Secret 10.

If you want to be happy, get holy!

SECRET 11

When you think you've arrived, it's time to start over.

Considering God made us, I've always assumed He must have a good sense of humor.

I hope so.

If we were sinners *in the hands of an angry God,* no one would escape the big barbecue in hell.

Praise the Lord for His good news in Jesus which is far more eternal than our bad news!

Here's a quick review from Paul:

The bad news - "All have sinned and fall short of the glory of God" (Romans 3:23).

The good news - "All are justified by His grace as a gift, through the redemption that is in Christ Jesus...The saying is trustworthy and deserving of full acceptance, that Christ Jesus came into the world to save sinners" (Romans 3:24; 1 Timothy 1:15).

Or as William Barclay noted in *The Mind of St. Paul* (1955), "The basic idea behind the conception of grace is the undeserved generosity of God."

R. C. Sproul has often expressed it this way to his students: "Pray for mercy; but don't pray for justice *because you may get it!*" There are two ways to look at God's grace: *grace is getting what we don't deserve* (heaven) and *grace is not getting what we deserve* (hell).

I learned this gospel from my first mentor and pastor

The Rev. Harold F. Mante back in Forty Fort, Pennsylvania's First United Presbyterian Church.

He'd always greet people, "Blessings on you."

When I asked what that means, he whispered, "I'm praying God treats you well even though you don't deserve it."

Blessings on you!

Always remember the good news is not how good we are or can become but how good He is as confirmed in Jesus.

We are not saved by our works of righteousness or *because of* who we are and what we do; but we are saved by the free and unmerited favor of God through faith in Jesus *in spite of* who we are and what we do.

That's why Jesus is *the Gospel.*

Getting back to humor, there's a story about Jesus walking around heaven and hearing an old man's voice. He asks, "Who is it?" The voice answers, "I'm just a poor old carpenter searching for my son." Jesus inquires, "Joseph?" The voice responds, "Pinocchio?"

That story reminds me of those high school reunions when everybody gathers to see how many faces from the past are still recognizable through older filters of kodachromed recollections.

While I know some folks are really *into* reunions, I've been to only one high school reunion and avoided every college, seminary, and post-graduate shindig.

I'm just not *into* them.

They resurrect old cliques, remind me of too many things that I'd rather delete from the hard drive of my noodle, and evoke the kind of nostalgia that recalls the 20s and 30s without depression, 40s and 50s without World

160

War II and Korea, and 60s and 70s without drugs, promiscuity, navel-gazing, and so on.

Besides, I don't need *reunions* to stay in touch with friends who remain connected by telephone, cyberspace (e-mail), post office (snail mail), automobile, and O'Hare.

I did go to my twentieth high school reunion on 1 September 1990. Everybody looked so old; and I continued to look through 18 year old eyes until a friend theorized, "I see you've got hair on your face to make up for the lack of it on your head."

Semi-truthfully, everybody looked pretty good; though I recollected more hair and waistlines under 123.

I thought of other things too; and some of them could get me into big trouble if I repeated them.

It was amusing.

Ellen was still a snob and pranced around like a double-meaning Queen "B."

Mike was still shy and sitting alone.

I was sure Mark hadn't forgiven David and me for tossing those cherry bombs down the other hole at scout camp while he was just sitting next to it and minding his own business.

Jackie told me Ruthie was looking for me; and I wondered how I would react.

I felt nothing.

I felt good about that.

So did my wife.

Eleven classmates were dead.

Vietnam. Drugs.

Alcohol. Cancer. Cars.

Broken hearts.

Suicide.

Mike told me his brother had snapped again and was back with their parents.

Bobby fried his brains and was *in* again.

Richard didn't come because his wife's ex-husband threatened to kill him if he showed up.

Marvin asked Esther, "So what's your last name this year?"

David still measured manhood by six-packs and pick-ups.

Some guy who I didn't remember greeted me like a good buddy, put his arm around my shoulder as Meatloaf's "Paradise by the Dashboard Light" blared in the background, and pined, "Life was so much simpler back then. Everything is so complicated anymore."

Maybe that's why people drink so much at reunions.

I don't know.

But I know if you're longing for the way things never were or maybe were but are no more, you'll keep going back for something as elusive as peace in the Middle East or loyalty in France.

So I've got a suggestion.

Have a reunion with Jesus.

There's nothing to lose except for some bad memories; and there's everything to gain when your class finally graduates.

The most apocalyptic moment of my life comes to mind.

I was a fifth grader at Lincoln Street School in Nanticoke, Pennsylvania.

As I was sitting in homeroom during lunch one day

and gobbling down my peanut butter and jelly sandwich while trying to trade an apple for a Hershey bar or Mallo Cup, I watched my homeroom teacher (Mr. Moore) take out his false teeth and gum graham crackers to death.

It was disgusting.

I forgot about the Hershey bar and Mallo Cup.

I looked over and saw Donna making eyes at me. Though I wasn't really a Cub Scout in heat and spent most of my time dreaming about pitching for the Yankees, we had a thing going on. She would give penny candy to me if I would go into the cloakroom and let her kiss me.

It was disgusting.

But after so many years of counseling miserable couples who sell out for a lot less, I look back and realize I was just learning some of the economics of gender relations.

I spotted Melvin squirming in his seat again; which meant he was about to make a puddle under his desk or expose himself to Tom and hope Muffie was watching.

Ernie was picking his nose as usual.

Bobby ripped off somebody else's Tastycakes.

And Marilyn, the first girl to cause my heart to flutter who was in her third year of fifth grade, started stroking my back.

I thought, "Everybody in here is so messed up."

Then it hit me in a startling experience of adolescent logic, "If *everybody* in here is messed up, then *I* must be messed up too."

Calvin's obsession with *total depravity* made sense from then on. It remains a turning point in my life.

I recognized the bad news of my life.

I also started to listen a little bit more to the good news in Sunday School.

I won't say it made any sense for a really good guy like Jesus to die for the sins of people like us who are always messing up.

But it surely helped me to understand why we call Him our *Savior.*

Such revelations of my sin and His saving grace through faith witness to Secret 11: "When you think you've arrived, it's time to start over."

No matter how good we were or are or can be, we're never quite good enough to make up for how bad we were, are, and will be every now and then.

Whenever we think we've got it all together, our carnalities pop up like a bad rap song and we plunge back into less than holy behaviors.

That's why I caution others and remind myself daily not to ride too high in the saddle. That's when we're easy targets; and that's when one little slip leads to a long fall down to earth.

When I was 29, I was called to be the senior pastor of one of our denomination's biggest churches.

It was heady stuff.

I had a big staff, good salary, perks galore, and never paid for lunch, golf, or traffic tickets.

But I'll never forget my interview by the presbytery committee responsible for approving the call.

The chairman shook my hand after I got through the committee and warned,

Well, Bob, you're a bright guy and you'll do just fine in the pulpit. Technically, I think you'll be O.K. But I voted against you and I'll tell you why. Let's say my 25 year old daughter came home and said she had just found the perfect man to be her husband; but he was only 12 or 13. Do you catch my drift?

I was so ticked!

I must have turned blood purple!

But he was right.

Intellectually, I was ready.

Emotionally and spiritually, I wasn't even close.

When the chairman told me I wasn't ready, I felt like reminding him that Jesus was supposedly 30 when he started to save the world.

I overlooked He was also *God.*

I thought I had arrived.

I hadn't.

I messed up.

It's Secret 11.

A missionary story out of China comes to mind.

Several members of a small church in a remote village went to the pastor and complained about the wife of a deacon who was stealing chickens from her neighbors. They told the pastor, "You've got to do something about it."

The very next Sunday, the pastor preached on the 8th commandment of God: "You shall not steal" (Exodus 20:15).

The deacon whose wife was stealing chickens said to the pastor after the service, "That was an excellent sermon."

A few days later, members of the church returned to the pastor and said, "That sermon didn't do any good at all. She's still stealing our chickens."

The very next Sunday, the pastor preached, "You shall not steal your neighbor's property."

The deacon whose wife was stealing chickens said to the pastor after the service, "That sermon was even better than last week's. You've really got to be specific with these people."

A few days later, members of the church returned to the pastor and said, "That sermon didn't do any good at all. She's still stealing our chickens."

The very next Sunday, the pastor preached, "You shall not steal your neighbor's chickens."

The deacon whose wife was stealing chickens rushed to the pastor after the service with veins popping from his red face and blasted, "Now listen, preacher, you're not supposed to be that specific in the pulpit!"

Everybody needs some of that salt that stings to heal every now and then.

Everybody needs to be stung with the truth about everybody's need for God to answer our *human* failures, foibles, and fallibilities with His gracious *divinity*.

Everybody needs a Virginia Damon in their lives.

She was my first speech teacher at Princeton.

She was tough.

She had been the acting coach for Jackie Gleason and Art Carney on *The Honeymooners.*

We called her VD.

After my first sermon in seminary, she called me to her office and said, "Well, you're not a basket case. We'll see what we can do."

It was a body punch to the conceit of a Princeton boy.

It was another reminder of how our Lord knocks us out of the saddle when we're riding too high.

I am convinced our Lord will do whatever it takes to humble us; because our Lord only uses *the poor in spirit* or those who recognize their dependence upon God for all things from here to eternity.

So watch out if you get a little too full of yourself in any way at any time with any person in whatever capacity.

There were two evil brothers who were very rich. They used their money to promote a public image that did not reflect their dark souls. They even attended the same church and were those proverbial weekend warriors who played the holy role in the sanctuary and betrayed their Lord in the streets of life by cheating and stealing their way to wealth.

During a capital campaign in the church to build a gymnasium for youth and expand the sanctuary, one of the brothers died.

The surviving brother handed a check to cover all expenses to the pastor. "I have only one condition," he said to the pastor, "you must say my brother was a saint at the funeral."

The next day at the funeral, the pastor who was known for being candid said, "He was an evil man. He cheated on his wife, abused his family, and did whatever it took to get to the top; but compared to his brother, he was a saint."

According to the New Testament, saints are women and men who love Jesus and love like Jesus to prove their love for Jesus as they trust Him for the eternal life that inspires confident living.

Sir James Simpson, the Edinburgh, Scotland doctor who discovered chloroform in 1847, understood how God's good news makes up for our bad news when we turn in humility to Him through faith in Jesus. When asked to name the most valuable discovery of his life, he shocked everybody in the lecture hall at the University of Edinburgh who expected him to mention the anesthetic chloroform which revolutionized surgery by confessing, "My most valuable discovery was when I discovered myself a sinner and that Jesus Christ was my Savior."

It's like the fellow who went to the gates of heaven and was greeted by Peter who asked for the password to enter. The man said, "Great is the Lord and greatly to be praised." "Good try, but that's not it," said Peter. So the man tried again, "God is love." "No," said Peter, "try again." "O.K.," the man said with increasing frustration, "How about John 3:16?" "No," said Peter, "but that was a really good try." "Well, if that's not it," the totally exasperated man finally sighed, "then I give up!" "That's it," said Peter, "Welcome!"

It's Secret 11.

I think of the fellow who asked, "Why can angels fly?" A mystic answered, "Because they take themselves lightly."

James explained, "God opposes the proud, but gives grace to the humble...Humble yourselves before the Lord, and He will exalt you" (see James 4).

A very skeptical smart aleck once scorned, "Does being born again mean you have two belly buttons?" I answered, "No, but it does mean God gives people who deserve to go to hell like you several second chances."

My friend Scott Merchant put it this way:

As long as Jesus is one of many options, He is no option.

As long as you can carry your burdens alone, you don't need a burden bearer.

As long as your situation brings you no grief, you will receive no comfort.

As long as you can take Him or leave Him, you might as well leave Him, because He won't be taken half-hearted.

But when you mourn, when you get to the point of sorrow for your sins, when you admit that you have no other option but to cast all your cares on Him, and when there is truly no other name that you can call, then cast all of your cares on Him, for He is waiting in the midst of the storm.

When you get to the end of yourself, you get to the beginning of God.

That's when you don't have to start all over again. That's when you've really arrived.

That's when you're saved.

Humbling yourself before the Lord is the path to His heights. It's Secret 11.

SECRET 12

**If you don't have calluses on your knees,
they're on your mind, heart, and soul.**

You may have heard about the priest, Pentecostal pastor, and rabbi who worked together as college chaplains. Scorning their cushy jobs of preaching to people, a student challenged them to preach to a bear. While exposing his studied ignorance, the student snipped, "It's easy to convert people with your preaching; but let's see how you do with real wildlife."

As if...

Well, that's for a Secret on reverse Darwinism

Taking up the challenge, the clergy headed into the woods to convert bears with their preaching.

The priest ended up on crutches with his arm in a sling. He reported, "When I began to teach the catechism to a bear, he started pounding on me; but after I sprinkled him with holy water, he settled down and prepared for confirmation and first communion."

The Pentecostal pastor ended up in a wheelchair. He reported, "When I tried to baptize a bear by immersion, he went berserk and pounced on me; but the Spirit filled me and I beat the hell out of him."

The rabbi ended up in the hospital. When the priest on crutches and Pentecostal pastor in a wheelchair went to visit, the rabbi asked, "Have you ever tried to circumcise a bear?"

Life can be tough.

Ruth and Jack Hoffman leave the tundra region of Northern Illinois every winter for Lake Havasu City, Arizona. Affirming those who say I write *in tongues,* they wrote to me on 12 March 2003, "Thanks for the card. Maybe by the time we get home, we'll figure out what it says."

Life can be tough.

A young woman returned home after a date. When her mother saw how sad her daughter looked, she asked, "What's wrong, honey?" The daughter sobbed, "Freddy proposed to me tonight; but he's an atheist and doesn't even believe in hell." "Now don't you worry yourself about that, darling," the mother counseled, "because as soon as you get married, I'll show him how wrong he is about that!"

Life can be tough.

Though every generation assumes its problems are much worse than its predecessors and successors, the truth is every generation has been plagued with meanness, madness, and misery since that *original sin* in the garden (see Genesis 3).

Rejecting God's will is the surest way to forfeit His existential favor.

I was a young boy dealing with teenage pathologies during the Cuban Missile Crisis in the early 60s.

I'd often pray like this before going to bed:

God, I would really appreciate it if You would make sure an A Bomb doesn't drop on my head any time soon. As You know, I want to pitch for the Yankees and I'm not quite ready yet. And I don't need to remind You that I'm really looking forward to getting my driver's license. And though I'm not really sure what the older boys are talking about during recess, I think I'd like to find out something about girls before the world blows up. I know this sounds kind of selfish, but I'm guessing lots of us are praying this way these days. Good night, Jesus. Amen.

Those were pretty immature prayers.

Isn't it great how we don't pray like that now that we're all grown up?

But life can still be tough.

Instead of A Bombs from the sky, we're praying about A Bombs in suitcases and planes flying into buildings and vials of whatever and...

Life can be tough.

Sometimes it's so overwhelming that we can't even articulate our prayers. Biblical texts like Psalm 6:6 and Romans 8:26 resonate in the deepest recesses of our often anxious hearts, minds, and souls:

I am weary with my moaning; every night I flood my bed with tears; I drench my couch with my weeping...the Spirit helps us in our weakness. For we do not know what to pray for as we ought, but the Spirit Himself intercedes for us with groanings too deep for words.

Prayer isn't as simple as it was when I was a young boy. My personal prayer list has far more daily additions than subtractions.

Can you relate?

When I approach pastoral prayers for worship, I realize the abridged version will have to suffice because folks prefer to go home before the evening news.

All of us know why Luther said he prayed at least three hours a day. Indeed, he said he prayed three hours on *regular* days; but if he was really busy, *he prayed six hours a day!*

173

As part of his occasional letter of encouragement called *Building One Another,* Dr. E. Stanley Ott, Senior Pastor of Pittsburgh, Pennsylvania's Pleasant Hills Community Church, wrote about spiritual discipline as the prerequisite to emotional, intellectual, and spiritual health in "Rhythms" (18 March 2003):

I visited an office building this week only to learn the elevator wasn't working.

Huffing and puffing with pounding heart as I climbed the stairs to the fifth floor, I realized how out of shape I was. I allowed the winter to interrupt my usual jogging workout and I can feel it.

Since then I've gone running twice. It's time I renew that rhythm in my life.

These weeks before Easter, the season of Lent, is a wonderful time to consider and renew the rhythms that sustain your life.

Do you have a devotional rhythm? I enjoy reading a Psalm, a chapter of the Old Testament and one from the New Testament each morning, followed by prayer. Find a devotional time and Bible reading and prayer pattern that fits you!

Are you practicing a rhythm in worship? Join God's people for worship every week that you are physically able to attend!

Do you have a rhythm in your close relationships? Years ago Charlie Shedd recommended dinner out once a week with your spouse (enjoy fellowship with a friend if you are single) and lunch once a month with each child. I have found it to be a wonderful practice.

Do you have a rhythm to your hospitality? Regularly invite into your life those you know well and those with whom new friendship is just beginning.

If we're not allowing *and making* time to approach our Lord's sovereign throne of grace through spiritual discipline (e.g., worship, prayer, Bible study, fasting, sacrament, silence, stewardship, and fellowship with believers), it won't be long before we become hopeless, restless, careless, *could-care-less,* and just about dead to Him, His, and ourselves.

It's Secret 12: "If you don't have calluses on your knees, they're on your mind, heart, and soul."

Prayer is hard work.

In our flushed, rushed, and razzle-dazzled world with calendars filling up quicker than dining rooms at Red Lobster and the Olive Garden after 4:30 p.m., we've got to schedule irretractable time for prayer as a divine appointment.

Yet even when we make time for prayer, we are often distracted from holy communion with Father, Son, and Holy Spirit.

Do you remember your last attempt to have some *quiet time?*

If you're like me, your heart drifted from God as your head was immediately cluttered with worldly cares and concerns about everything from grocery lists to credit card bills to what's for dinner to who is threatening global security this week.

Henri Nouwen understood such roadblocks to getting with God to get over life's challenges (*The Way of the Heart,* 1981):

> Just look for a moment at our daily routine. In general we are very busy people. We have many meetings to attend, many visits to make, many services to lead. Our calendars are filled with appointments, our days and weeks filled with engagements, and our years filled with plans and projects. There is seldom a period in which we do not know what to do, and we move through life in such a distracted way that we do not even take the time and rest to wonder if any of the things we think, say or do are *worth* thinking, saying or

doing. We simply go along with the many "musts" and "oughts" that have been handed on to us, and we live with them as if they were authentic translations of the Gospel of our Lord...

Solitude is the furnace of transformation. Without solitude we remain victims of our society and continue to be entangled in the illusions of the false self...

[Solitude]...is the place of conversion, the place where the old self dies and the new self is born, the place where the emergence of the new man and the new woman occurs...

As soon as I decide to stay in my solitude, confusing ideas, disturbing images, wild fantasies and weird associations jump about in my mind like monkeys in a banana tree...

The task is to persevere in my solitude, to stay in my cell until all my seductive visitors get tired of pounding on my door and leave me alone...

We enter into solitude first of all to meet our Lord and to be with Him and Him alone. Our primary task in solitude, therefore, is not to pay undue attention to the many faces which assail us, but to keep the eyes of our mind and heart on Him who is our Divine Savior.

That's why prayer is such hard work.

That's why the prayerful develop calluses in all the right places.

The prayerful are rewarded (Matthew 6:7-11):

Ask, and it will be given to you; seek, and you will find; knock, and it will be opened to you. For everyone who asks receives, and the one who seeks finds, and to the one who knocks it will be opened. Or which one of you, if his son asks him for bread, will give him a stone? Or if he asks for a fish, will give him a serpent? If you then, who are evil, know how to give good gifts to your children, how much more will your Father who is in heaven give good things to those who ask Him!

Or as James reported (5:13-18),

Is anyone among you suffering? Let him pray. Is anyone cheerful? Let him sing praise. Is anyone among you sick? Let him call for the elders of the church, and let them pray over him, anointing him with oil in the name of the Lord. And the prayer of faith will save the one who is sick, and the Lord will raise him up. And if he has committed sins, he will be forgiven. Therefore, confess your sins to one another and pray for one another, that you may be healed. The prayer of a righteous person has great power as it is working. Elijah was a man with a nature like ours, and he prayed fervently that it might not rain, and for three years and six months it did not rain on the earth. Then he prayed again, and heaven gave rain, and the earth bore its fruit.

When people think of John Calvin, images of a stiff, detached, anal, and intellectually tortured stoic come to mind.

While that helps explain why mainliners like Presbyterians claim him as their hero, it's a caricature that doesn't do justice to his total personality.

I think of how Calvin responded to the man who challenged, "If you know so much, tell us what God was doing before he created the heavens and the earth." Calvin snapped, "He was creating hell for the curious."

When asked why he wore a hat while preaching in Geneva's cathedral, he said, "It's cold in the cathedral *and there are pigeons.*"

Renowned for his theological acuity and often acerbic digressions in commentaries, lectures, and sermons, Calvin was notably pious. His life and ministry were guided by the simple sounding yet profound principle of "relying on His defense alone."

Calvin's contributions to the Kingdom were generated by spiritual discipline. He is a laudable illustration of Secret 12.

Kneeling or humbling one's self before God is the attitudinal prerequisite of productive prayer.

God blesses the humble.

Every once in a while, I take out my old *Nelson's Complete Concordance* (1957) and read all of the entries for humble, humbled, humbles, humbly, and humility as a spiritual discipline; and, invariably, I am driven to my knees in praise and thanks for how God's grace elevates anyone who will respect His sovereignty over existential and eternal life.

Here are some of the texts that have been particularly helpful in emphasizing this vertical relationship with its rewards for me:

Psalm 149:4 - "For the Lord takes pleasure in His people; He adorns the humble with salvation."

Proverbs 3:34 - "Toward the scorners He is scornful, but to the humble He gives favor."

Proverbs 11:2 - "When pride comes, then comes disgrace, but with the humble is wisdom."

Proverbs 22:4 - "The reward for humility and fear of the Lord is riches and honor and life."

Micah 6:8 - "He has told you, O man, what is good; and what does the Lord require of you but to do justice, and to love kindness, and to walk humbly with your God?"

Matthew 18:3-4 - "Truly, I say to you, unless you turn and become like children, you will never enter the Kingdom of Heaven. Whoever humbles himself like this child is the greatest in the Kingdom of Heaven."

Matthew 23:12 - "Whoever exalts himself will be humbled, and whoever humbles himself will be exalted."

James 4:6, 10 - "God opposes the proud, but gives grace to the humble...Humble yourselves before the Lord, and He will exalt you."

1 Peter 5:5-6 - "Clothe yourselves, all of you, with humility toward one another, for God opposes the proud but gives grace to the humble. Humble yourselves, therefore, under the mighty hand of God so that at the proper time He may exalt you."

I've always liked the definition of prayer crafted by the Westminster Divines: "Prayer is an offering up of our desires unto God, for things agreeable to His will, in the name of Christ, with confession of our sins, and thankful acknowledgment of His mercies" (*The Shorter Catechism* of 1647, Question 98).

My pastor and first mentor The Rev. Harold F. Mante told my confirmation class, "Prayer is *talking to and listening to* God."

Or as Simone Weil counseled as well as defined, prayer is "resolutely unmixed attention" to God.

It is *focused.*

Or as I heard Robert Schuller say many years ago, a person in prayer is like "a VW with an open sun roof."

Dr. Schuller's description of prayer points to the spiritual discipline urged upon disciples by Jesus in Gethsemane: "So, could you not watch with me one hour? Watch and pray that you may not enter into temptation" (Matthew 26:40-41).

That's why I understand prayer as "hanging out with God" or "making time to be with God."

The acronym ACTS has often been prescribed as a pattern for prayer:

Adoration of God's sovereignty as Father-Creator, saving Son Jesus, and enlightening, enabling, and sustaining Holy Spirit.

Confession of sins or how we reject God's will for our lives as exemplified in Jesus and explained in the Bible.

Thanksgiving for God's existential and eternal blessings.

Supplication or asking God's favor for others and ourselves.

Indisputably, the Lord's Prayer is the perfect pattern for prayer (Matthew 6:9-13).

Here's an abbreviated commentary:

"Our Father, who art in Heaven" - This is our appeal to the only One who is omnipotent, omniscient, and omnipresent; fully capable of caring for us from here to eternity.

"Hallowed be Thy name" - With God being holy, holy, holy (i.e., unparalleled as Almighty Sovereign), this expresses our desire to honor His holiness through thought, creed, and deed.

"Thy Kingdom come" - We long for His gracious reign in this world!

"Thy will be done; on earth as it is in Heaven" - God's will as profiled in Jesus and prescribed in the

Bible is obeyed perfectly in Heaven. We pray and labor for His will to be obeyed perfectly on earth.

"Give us this day our daily bread" - This recognizes our need and dependence upon God for physical and spiritual nourishment to keep keepin' on.

"And forgive us our debts; as we forgive our debtors" - We ask our Lord to wipe the slate clean of our sins against Him; noting the connection between our forgiveness of others and God's forgiveness of us. Indeed, this is the only part of the prayer which Jesus immediately annotated: "For if you forgive others their trespasses, your heavenly Father will also forgive you, but if you do not forgive others their trespasses, neither will your Father forgive your trespasses" (Matthew 6:14-15). This commentary can be expressed by simple equations: Forgiving = Forgiven, Unforgiving = Unforgiven, and Unforgiveness ≠ Forgiveness.

"And lead us not into temptation" - Knowing bad things taste good but lead to spiritual indigestion and disruption of our holy communion with the Lord, we ask His help to avoid anyone and anything that would distract or detour us from His paths of righteousness.

"But deliver us from evil" - Recognizing the strength and strategies of the source of all darkness in this world, we beg God's protection from and triumph over Satan (see Secret 8).

"For Thine is the Kingdom, and the power, and the glory, forever" - We know Almighty God is able to come through on all of the above for all of the below. History is *His* story and it will conclude with His ultimate, final, and everlasting victory.

"Amen" - That's our declarative assent to the preceding parts of the prayer. It's akin to saying, "That's right!" or "So be it!"

Let's return to the Westminster Divines' precise definition of prayer which highlights the humble attitude of productive prayer: "Prayer is an offering up of our desires unto God, *for things agreeable to His will...*"

Again, Jesus provided the perfect pattern of humility for prayer in Gethsemane: "My Father, if it be possible, let this cup pass from me; nevertheless, not as I will, but as You will" (Matthew 26:39). He wanted the cup to pass. He did not want to suffer. Yet Jesus subordinated His *wants* to the will of the Father.

He wanted the cup to pass *but it did not* because it was the will of the Father for the Son to suffer and die through crucifixion to enable resurrection and eternal life for all who will invite Him into their hearts as Lord and Savior.

Jesus submitted to the will of the Father because the basic axiom of life and eternity is *Father knows best.*

It's like Billy Graham's wife Ruth confessed, "God has not always answered my prayers. If He had, I would have married the wrong man several times."

God does answer every prayer.

Sometimes *yes.*

Sometimes *no.*

Sometimes *wait.*

God's answers to prayer are like a traffic signal:

When the light is green, we go!
When the *prayer is right*, God says, "Go!"
When the light is red, we stop!

When the *prayer is wrong,* God says, "Don't go!"
When the light is yellow, we wait!
When *God doesn't tell us to go or stop, we wait until
He tells us to go or stop!*

Sooner or later, we recognize *Father knows best.*
Or as Paul encouraged (see Romans 8),

**We know that for those who love God all things work
together For good, for those who are called according
to His purpose... If God is for us, who can be against
us? He who did not spare His own Son but gave
Him up for us all, how will He not also with Him
graciously give us all things?...Who shall separate
us from the love of Christ?...For I am sure
that...[nothing]... will be able to separate us from the
love of God in Christ Jesus our Lord.**

A troubled woman comes to mind:

A woman went to her rabbi and said, "O rabbi, life is so
terrible. God has forgotten me. Life is unbearable. My
husband goes off to work and leaves me alone with the
four children all day. He comes home but doesn't talk to
me. His mother and father came to live with us last week.
My mother and father came to live with us three months
ago. What can I do?"

The wise old rabbi responded, "Go to the barn, get the
horse, and bring the horse into the house."

With a puzzled look on her face, the woman asked,
"What kind of rabbi are you?"

"Child," the rabbi persisted, "just do as I say and come
back in a week."

"O rabbi," the woman said one week later, "that was
not good advice. All day long, I hear the clop, clop, clop of
the horse. That in addition to my mother and father and
his mother and father and the four children and a husband
who doesn't talk to me very much. Rabbi, you must help

me."

The wise old rabbi advised, "Go to the barn, get the cow, and bring the cow into the house."

"O rabbi," the increasingly exasperated woman blurted out, "you're not very helpful."

"Child," the rabbi counseled, "just do as I say and come back in a week."

"O rabbi," the woman said one week later, "that was not good advice. I cannot go on much longer with the horse and the cow and his mother and father and my mother and father and the four children and a husband who doesn't talk to me very much. Rabbi, you must help me."

The wise old rabbi instructed, "Put the horse and the cow back into the barn. Then come back in a week."

"O rabbi," the woman said one week later, "I feel so much better."

God's will may not be clear to us in all circumstances, but it's always right.

Discerning God's will often requires hard work.

It's Secret 12.

Predictably, someone will always say, "But I never hear God's voice? I never sense God is leading me."

That's because we are prone to talk too much and listen too little.

We've got to remember The Rev. Harold F. Mante's definition of prayer for young Christians: "Prayer is *talking to* and *listening to* God."

Prayer is hard work.

Prayer requires focusing on our relationship with the Lord.

Or, again, as a friend retorted when someone complained about the way he prayed, "Listen, lady, I wasn't talking to you anyway."

Prayer is holy communion with the Father through the Son as enabled by the Spirit to express our hearts with the expectation of guiding care.

Mother Teresa put it this way (*The Joy of Loving*, 1996), "How do we learn to pray? When Jesus was asked by His disciples how to pray, He did not teach them any methods or techniques. He said that we should speak to God as our Father, a loving Father."

It's the attitude not agenda brought to prayer that moves us into holy communion with God.

The prerequisite to productive prayer is a humility that believes *Father knows best* about all things at all times.

I'll never forget Jodie Harrison.

She was dying of cancer.

I was a young pastor who prayed with her for healing, anointed her with oil for healing according to the prescription of James 5:14-15, and revealed after sharing the sacrament together for the last time, "Jodie, I don't understand. I was sure our Lord would heal you. I don't understand why you're going home to Jesus right now."

She said, "I have been healed. For my entire adult life, I have prayed my family would be reconciled. My illness and imminent death have been used by God to restore my family. I am so happy. And besides, pastor, I'm going to heaven which is the greatest healing of all."

Yes, yes, yes, *Father knows* **best.**

Our continuing quest is to figure out God's will for our lives in order to live happily ever after.

That's why we pray.

It's hard work.

It's Secret 12.

Again, Martin Luther often said he prayed for three hours on most days; but if the day was especially busy and burdened, he prayed for six hours!

And as every spiritually disciplined person knows, the compensation far exceeds the efforts.

It's the Gospel.

Paul said it so well: "I consider that the sufferings of this present time are not worth comparing with the glory that is to be revealed to us" (Romans 8:18).

It's Secret 12.

SECRET 13

Energy and enthusiasm for Jesus confirm belief in Jesus;
the corollary being, *if you're not excited about Jesus,*
He doesn't show in your confession (what you say),
conduct (what you do), or countenance (how you appear).

As I mentioned as an illustration of Secret 2, I voted for Jimmy Carter when he ran against *never-elected-but-appointed-to-pardon-Nixon* President Gerald Ford in 1976.

My clergy friends used to joke, "America needs J.C."

He had a notoriously toothy smile, played softball, survived Admiral Hyman Rickover, grew peanuts, and taught Sunday School.

So I voted for him *once.*

When I discovered he had lived in Atlanta as a state senator at the same time as Martin Luther King, Jr. but followed the advice of handlers who urged distance from the Christocentric civil rights leader for fear of alienating rednecks which would have been political suicide, I began to doubt his storied "Christian" convictions. Playing *Mr. Born Again Christian President* after that stunt of assuaging bigots by sacrificing principles for political expediency seems rather hypocritical.

It wasn't encouraging to watch him stand by so impotently as Iran's Islamic nutball Ayatollah Ruhollah Khomeini nodded to the seizure of our embassy in Tehran by his disciples who took 66 American hostages. It took the election of President Ronald Reagan to clean up that mess.

He continued to play softball when the USSR invaded Afghanistan; pathetically "punishing" them by prohibiting America's participation in the Moscow Olympics of 1980.

Nevertheless, he remains a nice guy who builds houses for the poor through Habitat for Humanity and has a Nobel Peace Prize to prove it; though, again, knowing Yasser Arafat also picked up that check causes one to wonder what that's worth.

Sadly, he's been whining about the inadequacies of successors ever since his butt-whipping by President Reagan (1980) who restored the domestic pride and international respect shattered by Presidents Carter, Ford, Nixon, and Johnson.

And throughout the early months of 2003, he went on and on and on about President Bush's "unjust" war on Iraq.

Reading his guest editorials and watching cameos on fawning talk shows, I'm reminded of President Reagan who said during a debate with the soon-to-be former President Carter, "There he goes again!"

President Carter's understanding of the constitution of a just war is as weak as his record in the White House.

It resurrects the joke that started going around not long after his inauguration: "Do you know what's in a Jimmy Carter sandwich? *A little peanut butter and lots of baloney!*"

While I have had a hard time tracing President Carter's just war theory back to its reputed author Augustine or even renowned just war commentator Roland Bainton without even comparing Michael Novak, he has prompted me to review a few appropriate Biblical texts:

1. Romans 12:18 - "So far as it depends on you, live peaceably with all." It's *Golden Rule Living:* "Whatever you wish

that others would do to you, do to them" Matthew 7:12). But as the lamb said to the lion, "O.K., but you lie down first!" Or as I learned one Friday evening as a high school freshman, it takes two to dance.

2. Psalm 120:7 - "I am for peace, but when I speak, they are for war!" That's the cold reality of life in this world. It only takes one to start a fight. Unless we adopt a pacifist's mentality which includes allowance for the slaughter of others not as ideologically committed, sometimes conflict is unavoidable no matter how hard we try.

3. Jeremiah 6:14 - "They have healed the wound of my people lightly, saying, 'Peace, peace,' when there is no peace." Or as President Reagan said, "There he goes again!" Pollyannas reincarnating Neville Chamberlain may appeal to our bleeding hearts, but their attempts at being rational with the irrational is illogical in the face of those diabolical forces in this world determined to dominate and destroy.

4. Psalm 34:14 - "Seek peace and pursue it." Our goal is to enable life, liberty, and the pursuit of happiness for everyone. But if someone is determined not to allow that for everyone, peace can mean praying *and working* to inhibit that someone from threatening everyone. That's why Jesus said, "Blessed are the peacemakers" (Matthew 5:9). To *seek peace and pursue it* may necessitate restraining those who do not share this ethic. I must add that Biblical faith understands the most efficacious path to peace being through Jesus who emphasized loving each other as proof of loving God (e.g., John 13:34).

That's why I have supported President Bush's war on Iraq.

Charles Colson said it well in "The Moment of Truth" (*Breakpoint,* 18 March 2003): "The just war doctrine, in my opinion, applies most clearly to Iraq. The doctrine of just war, we must remember, flows out of the Christian command to love your neighbor. It is an act of love to wield the sword against evil and against threats to innocent lives. A justly fought war against Saddam Hussein will be...just a war."

I think of Lutheran pastor Dietrich Bonhoeffer who conspired to assassinate Adolf Hitler because he concluded it was not only his responsibility to care for the victims of a mad motorist but also to do all in his power to remove the madman from the wheel.

No one in her or his right mind wants war.

But no one in her or his right mind does not try to stop butchers like Adolf Hitler and Saddam Hussein.

Unless you are some kind of navel-gazing neo-isolationist who only cares about national security, which is tantamount to saying to hell with everybody else, you are compelled to *pursue* peace.

Regrettably but realistically, war becomes peace-making when it's the only way to exorcise evil.

It's always so nauseating to hear intellectually inconsistent and theologically illiterate clergy, churchgoers, celebrities, journalists, and all the rest bellowing against America's pursuit of peace by going to war to free oppressed people and exorcise hosts and exporters of terror. I'm convinced they must be related to the German "Christians" who so shamelessly turned the other way as Jews and so many others were carted off to ovens by the Nazis.

It's absolutely antithetical to our ethic to suggest we should not intervene "over there" because we are not being affected "over here" or that we should not intervene "over there" because it *could* cause us to be affected "over here."

When did Christianity lose its active concern for the world?

When did *self*ishness and *self*-absorption and *self*-interest become parts of our ethic?

When did *my rights, my needs, and my concerns* become more faithful to Jesus and the Bible than committing our resources and securities to protect, preserve, and promote the rights, needs, and concerns of others?

When I hear intellectual and theological dolts reincarnate and reinvent Jesus as some kind of Tiny Tim tiptoeing through the tulips and getting all beside Himself because some saints have the guts to go out into the world and stop butchers like Hitler and Hussein, I ask if they really think Jesus would take their cozy-armchair-retire-to-Starbucks-after-discussion-group approach of doing little else but *rapping* or *dialoging* or *pontificating* or *uttering moral outrage* at the evil works of evil people.

Can you hear the rooster crowing?

I guess some folks feel comfortable washing their hands with Pilate. It's much safer to get your nails done than hands dirty or even nail-scarred.

When did Christianity lose its active concern for the world?

"Christianity" didn't get it from Jesus. He said (Matthew 28:16-20; Acts 1:8),

All authority in heaven and on earth has been given to me. Therefore go and make disciples of all nations, baptizing them in the name of the Father and of the Son and of the Holy Spirit, and teaching them to obey everything I have commanded you. And surely I am with you always, to the very end of the age...You will be my witnesses in Jerusalem, and in all Judea and Samaria, and to the ends of the earth.

Jesus never said, "To hell with the world as long as you're safe and secure and snuggly and not being hassled."

He commanded us to love *the world*. Navel-gazing-me-and-Jesus-to-hell-with-everybody-else religion always pops up like a spiritual zit whenever we forget personal salvation compels corporate responsibilities.

Never forget how Jesus connected personal salvation with corporate responsibilities (e.g., Matthew 20:26-28; 25:31-46; John 3:16-17; 15:13):

> **Whoever would be great among you must be *your* servant, and whoever would be first among you must be *your* slave, even as the Son of Man came not to be served but to serve, and to give His life as a ransom for many...As you do it for others, you do it for me...For God so loved the world, that He gave His only Son, that whoever believes in Him should not perish but have eternal life. For God did not send His Son into the world to condemn the world, but in order that the world might be saved through Him...Greater love has no one than this, that someone lays down his life for his friends.**

The parable of the good Samaritan is instructive (Luke 10:25-37). The story highlights the indiscriminate character of Christian *agape* love. A man in need is helped without reference to color, culture, creed, socioeconomics, or any other prejudicially segregating factor. Jesus concluded with this stern command to anyone who claims Him as *Lord* as well as Savior, "You go, and do likewise" (Luke 10:37).

Paul expressed the connection between salvation and service this way: "If you confess with your mouth that Jesus is Lord and believe in your heart that God raised Him from the dead, you will be saved" (Romans 10:9).

It's Secret 13: "Energy and enthusiasm for Jesus confirm belief in Jesus; the corollary being, *if you're not excited about Jesus, He doesn't show in your confession (what you say), conduct (what you do), or countenance (how you appear)."*

Paul's understanding of the connection between salvation and service *or the behavior that confirms belief* is clear, concise, and conclusive.

He talks about "confessing with your mouth" after "believing in your heart."

That means the *inward conviction* of Jesus as Lord and Savior is confirmed by the *outward expression* of discipleship as profiled in Jesus and prescribed in the Bible.

Putting it another way, what we do confirms what we believe and that completed faith determines our ultimate destiny.

Or as Calvin stated, we *show* the signs of our salvation. We could reduce this to a simple formula:

Christianity = Belief in Jesus + Behavior like Jesus

It's Secret 13.

When we are authentic Christians, we pray and work and try our best to confirm our creeds with deeds because we are so excited about His eternal and existential blessings and the privilege to advance His Kingdom *on earth as it is in heaven.*

We *want* to walk (behavior) the talk (belief).

Conversely, if we are not authentic Christians, our walk will contradict our talk.

A young woman in New Jersey comes to mind.

She was a rather serious sort in her 30s who had attended worship services regularly before I arrived.

She stopped coming within the first year of my installation as pastor of Clark, New Jersey's Osceola Presbyterian Church.

Trained to focus on the immediate needs of the church, I never got around to asking why she stopped. Besides, one of the biggest mistakes of churches is expending too much energy on inactive members instead of the faithful and inquiring friends.

Providentially, I ran into her at a grocery store. Figuring it wasn't the time or place to be prophetic if not pastoral, I went the innocuous conversation route.

She took a different direction and said, "I've wanted to call you and explain why I don't come to church anymore."

I held my breath.

She continued, "I used to have the whole pew to myself. There are too many people now. I want it to be like it used to be – just me and Jesus."

It was one of the saddest and most selfish things that I've ever heard. She wanted Jesus *just for herself.*

Maybe that explains why some churches aren't very inviting. They emit the odor of exclusion.

They don't want to share space or Jesus.

They like their *small*ness - actually and attitudinally. Essentially, such folks are announcing, "To hell with everybody else."

Songs like "I Love to Tell the Story" and "We've a Story to Tell to the Nations" must seem like glossolalia to them.

Certainly, they do not understand discipleship includes embracing *and enfleshing* our Lord's passion for including everyone in the family of faith.

It's a fundamental principle of discipleship: *inward conviction* is confirmed by *outward expression;* and the lack of *outward expression* exposes the fraud of *inward conviction*

Simply, talk without walk is *baloney.*

I'm reminded of a favorite story which I *try* not to tell on Christmas Eve or Easter Day because I don't want to offend anyone who is concerned about me offending anyone who has no conscience about offending God:

A man approaches the pearly gates and Peter asks, "Why should we let you in?"

The man says, "Well, I went to church on Christmas Eve and gave five dollars."

Gabriel checks the big book and says, "That's right, Peter, he went to church on Christmas Eve and gave five dollars."

"What else?" Peter asks the man.

"Well," the man continues, "I went to church on Easter Day and gave five dollars."

Gabriel checks the big book and says, "That's right, Peter, he went to church on Easter Day and gave five dollars."

"What else?" Peter asks the man.

Becoming a bit anxious, the man says, "I didn't know I had to do anything more than show up in church on Christmas and Easter and throw a few dollars into the bucket."

Peter asks Gabriel, "What should we do?"

The wise old angel pauses, strokes his beard, closes the book, and answers, "I say we give him his ten dollars back and tell him to go to hell."

Christians don't worry about such pejorative possibilities because they walk the talk.

Christians *act* saved.

You may have heard about the traveling salesman who knocked on a door. "Come in," a voice called. When the salesman went into the house, he saw the voice coming from a parrot; but also noticed two big Dobermans inching toward him with froth dripping from their snarling mouths. "Come in," repeated the parrot. "Listen, you dumb parrot," the extremely frightened salesman asked, "is that all you can say?" "No," the parrot replied, "sic 'em boys!"

Or as I used to tell my preaching students back at Kansas City's Nazarene Theological Seminary in the early 80s, "Jesus told us to be fishermen. That means were supposed to *hook 'em* for Jesus."

The *outward expression* of our *inward conviction* is seen through our confession (what we say), conduct (what we do), and countenance (how we appear):

Confession "In golf as in life," wrote Jeff Rude for *Golfweek* (19 October 2002), "it's best to make little decisions with your head and big decisions with your heart." That was the difference between Saul and David: "The Lord has sought out a man after His own heart" (1 Samuel 13:14). If we've got a heart for God, meaning our totality (emotions, intellect, spirit, and body) is dedicated to Him, we pray and labor to say what He would say and do what He would do as profiled in Jesus and prescribed in the Bible.

Conduct - A rabbi told my friend Jim Tuckett, "When you don't know the right thing to do, do that which is least wrong." Or as Nike advertises, "Just do it!" It's like the late Dr. James I. McCord, the late President of Princeton Theological Seminary and The World Alliance of Reformed Churches, often told seminarians, "I don't care what you do, but do something. For God's sake, do something with your lives and ministries." While we endeavor to *do something* consistent with Christological and Biblical revelation, sometimes we do our best and ask God's mercy for the rest.

Countenance - Some folks look like Jesus is still dead and buried. I think of the fellow who said, "I was thinking about being a preacher, but too many of them looked and sounded like undertakers." Again, "If you're happy and you know it, then you really ought to *show* it." If you're repelling more than compelling people to turn to Jesus, it's time to check out your *inward conviction* because what's on the inside is being seen on the outside.

I'll never forget Leroy Holmes

Oral Robert introduced him to me.

He combined confession, conduct, and countenance into a contagious and compelling witness for Christ.

Though I don't know if he ever completed high school, I know he didn't go to Princeton!

He was a *get down* preacher man.

Whenever he preached, people would start getting into it: "Yes, yes, yes...Go on!...That's right!"

He wasn't like mainline preachers who show up in Spirit-moving churches. When they preach, you'll hear folks pleading, "Help him, Jesus!...Jump on him, Jesus!...Fill him, Jesus!"

Oral Robert took me to a service at his church which I will never forget.

Blacks, whites, yellows, browns, rich, poor, cops, convicts, hookers, hooked, and all of the below gathered to hear the Gospel through this exceedingly energetic and enthusiastic but under-educated evangelist for Jesus.

He couldn't put two sentences together without obliterating Elizabethan English:

> We lives in a terrible world...Praise Jesus!
> Peoples are stealing from each other...Hallelujah, Jesus!
> I tellin' you womens are being raped in the streets...Thank You, Lord!
> Killins' and adulteries and drugs and booze....Praise the Lord!

While none of it made much sense to me from an arrogant *MLA Style Sheet* or *Gregg Reference Manual* perspective, all of the Christians were with him because he was with Him. People were praising God and coming alive in the Lord and preparing to return to the world transformed by the Word.

Conversely, our world is filled with educated clergy whose passion for Jesus, if dynamite, wouldn't be enough to blow their noses.

But if you've got a heart for God like that under-educated preacher in New Jersey who was smart enough to depend upon God and point people to Jesus, then the omnipotent, omniscient, omnipresent, Creator, Savior, and Sustainer will take your mustard seed brain and use you to help convert the world to Him.

Someone said, "Man can live for about forty days without food, and about three days without water, about eight minutes without air,...but only for one second without hope."

People who are alive in Jesus draw people into *Son*shine. It's Secret 13.

My friend Eric Ritz, Pastor of Schuylkill Haven, Pennsylvania's First United Methodist Church, told this story to his congregation on 5 March 2003 (Ash Wednesday):

> A balloon vendor was entertaining children. He was filling the balloons with helium and letting them rise to the sky - a red one, a blue one, a green one, a white one. He felt a tug on his pants leg; and it was a little African-American boy who said, "Mister, if you would let a black balloon go, would it rise to the sky as well?" The man said, "Son, it is not the color of the balloon that matters. It is not what is on the outside of the balloon. It is what is on the inside of the balloon that makes it rise to the sky."

When our hearts are filled with Jesus, we rise with Him; and everyone around us is uplifted.

SECRET 14

Corporate Christians (apostate, moderate, and evangelical) have just enough of Jesus to feel comfortable about themselves (i.e., spiritually anesthetized) but not enough to be any real good for God's sake; knowing true discipleship puts personal and vocational securities at risk.

My two closest friends in seminary were Paul Swedlund and Paul Watermulder.

Paul Watermulder has been Senior Pastor of Burlingame, California's First Presbyterian Church for a few decades. He followed Tom Gillespie who left Burlingame to become President of Princeton Theological Seminary.

Paul Swedlund is dead. He fell off a Colorado mountain on 17 August 1994 and went home to Jesus after about a decade as Pastor of Kansas City, Missouri's Northminster Presbyterian Church.

Just before the memorial service at Kansas City's Colonial Presbyterian Church, Paul Watermulder and I compared notes. Simultaneously, we said, "I wonder who will do the next service."

Even more painful than Paul's passing – *believing in his eternal life yet stunned by an assumed "premature" death has meant the mingling of mourning and joy since our existential separation* – was greeting John Barco after the memorial service.

I had not seen John for a long time. He chaired the search committee which called Paul to Northminster. I had

201

recommended Paul to them; and because it turned out to be a good match, they thought well of me.

John was crying uncontrollably. He wrapped his arms around me and sobbed, "I'm having a really hard time with this. You probably don't know that Paul took a lot of shots from these people every day. They made life miserable for him so often. And here they are..."

His voice trailed off.

I thank God that we didn't talk before I preached at the memorial service for one of my best friends.

I guess I shouldn't have been surprised.

It goes with the turf.

I've often said to agitate the guilty, "If you'd like to know what it's like to be a pastor, put on a deerskin and go walking through the woods on the first day of hunting season."

I recall my Freudian professor at Drew Uniersity who told our doctoral study group, "The problem people in your church are unsually constipated. That's why they dump on you."

After so many years in "professional" ministry, my hard drive is filled with painful stories – stories of pastors who have been hated while trying to love like Jesus. Putting it another way, I've got lots of stories about pastors who have been hated *in a Christian kind of way* by churchgoers.

Yeah, nobody's perfect; not even those self-appointed clerical abusers who waltz around in a thinly- veiled attempt to divert attention from their own emotional, intellectual, and spiritual dysfunctions by transferring them from the pew to the pulpit. It's like an older elder once warned, "The best way to make sure nobody sees your house is burning down is to start a fire in somebody else's backyard."

I've seen it all through the years.

A former preaching student wrote,

As you know, I definitely felt led of the Lord to come out here. Lately, however, I have seriously believed He is telling me to pack my bags. There is one family that has caused me a fair amount of grief. There is nothing unusual about that, because you warned us that it is a problem inherent with the pastorate. Their charges: I eat in fancy restaurants. I tell them being a Christian is more important than being a Nazarene.

A recently ordained fellow is thinking of leaving the ministry because people who have been picking and pecking away at his humanity have started digging up dirt from his past and passing it around without any regard for Christianity's redemptive themes. His spirit is being systematically crushed as his humanity is being demonized.

A friend has poured out his heart, soul, mind, body, *and family* for his rapidly growing congregation and has been rewarded with this evaluation: "You can ask us for more money. We'll say no. Then you can go looking for a bigger church."

Another friend was courted passionately by his calling church. *They wanted him so much.* Once he arrived, the congregation reserved affection and affirmation for his immediate predecessor. He ended up looking for affection and affirmation in all the wrong places. They threw him out and his presbytery defrocked him.

The pastor of one of our denomination's largest and most influential churches resigned a few years ago.

Though only a few years from retirement, he entered the pulpit one Sunday and told the truth which only a few had known but kept to themselves for so long. He recalled years of pain in a marriage of unmet needs. He talked about the absence of love in his life. Then he confessed falling in love with another woman.

He resigned on the spot.

Though there is never acceptable rationalization for behavior antithetical to Biblical revelation, he was right for confessing he was wrong.

A congregational meeting was held not long after that.

Person after person got up to vent their frustrations and angers about their fallen leader. He had let them down and nobody seemed willing to pick him up.

Finally, a lawyer stood and said,

I am a lawyer by trade. My job has always been to find faults and place blame. In this case, I speak as a parishioner in support of a pastor, who has always been there for us regardless of our faults. When we have been arrested for a DUI, found in bed with the wrong person, fired with cause, accused of abusive behavior, found with one hand in the corporate cookie jar, and caught in sin, our pastor has always been there for us. He has been there in love, offering the grace of God, and embracing us despite our sin. I do not understand why we cannot be here for him, as he was there for us.

The rules, of course, are different for clergy.

So he was rejected, condemned, and abandoned.

Is it any wonder why the unchurched, agnostics, and atheists condemn churches for failing to practice what they preach?

Funny how the talk of redemption is rarely enfleshed by the church.

We shoot our wounded.

We discard those who are in sin rather than embracing and guiding them back to wholeness through Christocentric and Biblical fidelity. But, then again, look what they did to Him!

I guess the apple doesn't fall far from the tree.

A pastor about to retire wrote to me:

> I'm glad I'm getting out. All people do in the church today is bitch, bitch, bitch. The bitchiness of the world has poisoned the church and nobody has the guts to do anything about it. I've served on ministerial committees for years and pastors are always blamed and end up paying the cost...I've never seen a member held responsible for anything...I'll tell you, Bob, I'm glad I'm getting out.

It's like the elder who reassured the guy who hated me *in a Christian kind of way* in my first church, "It's O.K., Carl, preachers come and go, but we stay."

That's why I've been campaigning for executive presbyters, district superintendents, bishops, and the like to exercise ecclesiastical discipline with the increasing number of irregular people in today's churches who live to create hell for priests, pastors, elders, deacons, and anyone else called into church leadership.

I believe it's time for ecclesiastical authorities to stop playing footsies with the devil and identify and isolate troublemakers. If we can dissolve pastoral relationships and defrock clergy, we can resurrect excommunication to deal with destructive, divisive, and diabolically motivated members.

Fair is fair.

Right is right.

Identifying and isolating poison keeps it from infecting the whole body (see Secret 8).

Inevitably, whenever I write or talk about this plague, some folks assume I'm just venting about my own problems; abandoning professional objectivity for personal pathos.

While I have been wounded over the years (deserving and otherwise), I haven't had too much to complain about.

Currently, I'm not among those 75% of America's clergy who would relocate tomorrow for a better financial, ideological, or relational deal.

Besides, I have developed a spiritual survival strategy which has enabled me to live and minister joyfully on bad as well as good days.

I cherish my family and friends.

I have a positive addiction (golf) which is a lot cheaper than a shrink and safer than narcotics.

I write.

I'm old enough to know, as a Southern gentlewoman suggested to me years ago, "If they're nippin' at your heels, they're behind you."

I've been in the business long enough to know how to identify and isolate the irregular without them knowing it.

As my daddy taught, "You can tell people to go to hell in a way that they're looking forward to the trip."

I can sniff out "I've-got-lots-of-problems-but-I-refuse-to-acknowledge-them-I'll-pretend-you're-the-problem" transference.

I rarely react to the first thing that anyone says. That's just an attention-getter. Usually, it's the second thing that's important. It's like a watch. If there's a problem, don't look at the hands. *Look deeper!*

I know it's a short list of people who will really care when the roll is called up yonder for me. I've often said if

I die after Sunday's sermon, there will be ham and cole slaw in the church hall on Wednesday and a congregational meeting the following Sunday to elect the next pastor search committee.

I'm becoming wiser as a serpent (tough-minded) and less gentle as a dove (tender-hearted).

I've got calluses.

But what (*Who*) really saves me is inviting Jesus into my heart as Lord and Savior *every* day.

I depend upon Him for my existential as well as eternal survival within the context of His promise through the Psalmist, "Those who love me, I will deliver...I will protect those who know my name" (see. Psalm. 91)

Secret 1 is in heart and mind and soul at the beginning, during, and end of every day.

I look forward to that pie-in-the-sky; but just a taste here and now keeps me up when the meanness, madness, and misery of life in the modern world tries to push me down.

I live by taking the advice of a preaching professor: "Trust Jesus and, in everything else, hang loose.!"

A story from friend Walter Scott who went home to Jesus on 27 January 2002 is so true:

A banjo-picker died and went to heaven. Saint Peter said, "A banjo-picker? And bluegrass at that. With a background like that, you'll have to take a special test for admission. The test is simple. What is God's first name?" The banjo-picker said, "That's easy. God's first name is Andy. We sang it at Sunday School every week: 'Andy walks with me. Andy talks with me. Andy tells me I am His own...' "

To a few super-sophisticated scholastics, that hymn - "In the Garden" – is too anthropomorphic; but it's a spiritually supportive reality to anyone who invites Jesus into the heart as saving Lord *daily*.

"The woman who had been subject to bleeding for twelve years" comes to mind (Matthew 9:20-22). She "came up behind Him and touched the edge of His cloak. She said to herself, 'If I only touch His cloak, I will be healed.' "

She knew getting *in touch* with Jesus is the only way to experience wholeness, happiness, joy, and eternal security.

Jesus confirmed her confidence: "Take heart, daughter, your faith has healed you."

"And the woman," Matthew reported, "was healed from that moment."

That's how I have survived over the years.

I stay *in touch* with Jesus.

Jesus saves me.

Hebrews 12:2 is our counsel: "Let us fix our eyes on Jesus."

I try to assimilate the advice which I offered my preaching students: "When you preach, you shouldn't care what anybody but Jesus thinks about your sermon. If what you say pleases Him, that should be enough for now. It will be enough *in the end*."

Or as Mother Teresa implored, "Let us free our minds from all that is not Jesus."

An excessively intense man approached Mother Teresa and stated, "My vocation is to work for the lepers. I want to spend all my life, my everything in this vocation." She corrected, "You are making a mistake, brother. Your vocation is to belong to Jesus. He has chosen you for Himself and the work is only a means of your love for Him in action." She concluded, "Therefore it does not matter what work you are doing, but the main thing is that you belong to Him, that you are His and that He gives you the means to do this for Him."

Surely, there are many days that are anything but hot fudge sundaes. An older pastor once said to me, "Just one flea can make a big dog itch." Or as I've also heard, "You don't learn much from the second kick of a mule."

There are days when I thoroughly relate to the man who said to his wife, "I'm never going back to that church. Nobody likes me. They always criticize me. They blame me for everything. I feel like a scapegoat for all of their problems. If you can come up with one good reason to go back, I'll go back." She replied, "I've got two reasons for you to go back. First, you know it's the right thing to do. Second, you're the pastor."

The Lord compels the called to continue.

It's *irresistible.*

The Lord enables and encourages the called to continue by His saving grace.

Again, Jesus saves.

Mother Teresa said it so well:

Where Jesus is—there is joy
there is peace
there is love.

And that is why He made Himself the Bread of Life to be our love and joy.

No one else can give what He gives and He is there all the time.

We have only to realize that.

Candidly after so many years of ordained ministry, I can't figure out why anyone would want to be a pastor or "go into ministry" in any form or *fashion.*

Apart from the *irresistible* call, anyone who *wants* to be a pastor has some serious mental problems which should preclude her or him from consideration.

Considering the amount of education and hassles to *merit* ordination, the pay and hours are awful; and churchgoers persist in their twisted idea that they can say the kinds of things to clergy that clergy can't say without being reprimanded or removed from office.

Pearl comes to mind.

She made an appointment to say how much she hated my beard *in a Christian kind of way.*

I have never asked to see anyone to say her or his perfume stinks, personality sucks, or wild horses dragging me by the tongue couldn't persuade me to share intimacies.

Regardless, I quickly realized she was transferring pathologies connected to the dysfunctional relationship with her *bearded son* to me. In a moment of youthful pastor naiveté, I said I would shave it off if it would improve our shaky relationship.

She accepted my offer.

Though there are notable exceptions (see Secret 6), I am a man of my word; hence, I shaved off my beard reluctantly.

When I saw her approaching me after worship the following Sunday, I expected a warm greeting with proper gratitude.

Instead, she took my hand between her hands, patted it in a nauseatingly patronizing way, tilted her head, and said through a sickeningly syrupy smile not far from a scowl, "Now about your moustache."

Such episodes are common to all clergy who don't find them as funny as the churchgoers who script them.

Now that the years left in ministry aren't nearly as many as those spent, I admit I'd do it all over again; not because I've always liked my vocation but because it's who I am and what God has called me to be and do.

With *all of the above* as well as *all of the below* in mind, I often ask seminarians, "If this doesn't work out, what are your other vocational options?"

If they have other options, I know they're not *called* into pastoral ministry.

Pastoral ministry is not a choice.

It's an *irresistible* call by God.

The costs are so high and the challenges are so many that half-heartedness or double-mindedness will guarantee a career of disappointment, disillusionment, and depression without the occasional oasis of warm fulfillment.

That's why so many professional-without-being-called clergy self-destruct, quit, demit, lose their faith, or just go through the motions, pick up a check, and pile up pension credits.

Only if a person is called to ministry does our Lord provide the wherewithal to survive and press on with the vocation's missionary agenda "that at the name of Jesus every knee should bow, in heaven and on earth and under the earth, and every tongue confess. that Jesus Christ is Lord, to the glory of God the Father" (Philippians 2:10-11).

You may have heard about the elderly woman who returned home, found a burglar in the house, and yelled, "Stop! Acts 2:38!"

Acts 2:38 reads, "Repent and be baptized...in the name of Jesus Christ, for the forgiveness of your sins."

Getting back to the story, the burglar stopped and froze;

and the woman calmly called the police who came and arrested the man.

As the burglar was being interrogated at the station, an officer asked why he stopped when the woman quoted from the Bible. He snapped, "The Bible wasn't a problem. She said she had *an ax* and *two 38s!*"

Whenever I need a compelling cause to continue in ministry, I go back to why I became a pastor:

> I became a pastor because I felt *and was told* I have a gift for pointing out the positively inclusive benefits of accepting, affirming, and applauding Jesus as personal Lord and Savior.

> I became a pastor because I believe people need help through the church to experience and express their relationship with Jesus as Lord and Savior. I do not believe most churchgoers fit into Kurt Vonnegut's conclusion about people attending worship services to "daydream about God" with "sweetly faked attention" and no desire for sprinkling salt and reflecting His light.

> I became a pastor because I am positive about Jesus with enthusiasm and without reservation or equivocation yet Calvinistic about human motives and potential (review Secrets 2 and 6).

> I became a pastor because I like a Lord who insists people who claim to be His followers must give away their excess to the poor and get along with more than pretty people.

> I became a pastor because I believe the only hope for intrapersonal, interpersonal, and global peace is learning to love like Jesus – invitationally, inclusively, mercifully, selflessly, sacrificially, and unconditionally.

> I became a pastor to preach, teach, write about the struggle to be faithful to Jesus in the modern world, visit and pray with the hospitalized, enable spiritual formation, and prove you don't have to hide your humanity to be a part of the Kingdom.

I did not become a pastor to say nothing eloquently to insure personal and vocational securities, pander to popular prejudices, trumpet exclusionary theology, or waste precious time away from family, friends, and saints with ecclesiastical game players who transform our mission into a business or game of Monopoly.

I did not become a pastor to accommodate anyone who acts like Jesus is still dead and buried.

I became a pastor in the spirit of Colossians 3 and Hebrews 12: "Seek the things that are above, where Christ is...Let us fix our focus on Jesus."

I became a pastor *because* of Jesus: "Everyone who hears these words of mine and acts on them will be like a wise man who built his house on rock" (Matthew 7:24-27).

If you'll pardon the melodramatics and spiritualization, Bob Seger's 'Like a Rock" has always pumped me up:

> Stood there boldly
> Sweatin' in the sun
> Felt like a million
> Felt like number one
> The height of summer
> I'd never felt that strong
> Like a rock
>
> I was 18
> Didn't have a care
> Workin' for peanuts
> Not a dime to spare
> But I was lean and
> Solid everywhere
> Like a rock
>
> My hands were steady
> My eyes were clear and bright
> My walk had purpose

My steps were quick and light
And I held firmly
To what I felt was right
Like a rock
Like a rock -
I was strong as I could be
Like a rock -
Nothin' ever got to me
Like a rock - I was somethin' to see
Like a rock

And I stood arrow straight
Unencumbered by the weight
Of all these hustlers and their schemes
I stood proud - I stood tall
High about it all
I still believed in my dreams

20 years now-
Where'd they go
20 years
I don't know
I sit and I wonder sometimes
Where they've gone

And sometimes late at night
When I'm bathed in the firelight
The moon comes callin' a ghostly white
And I recall...I recall

Like a rock - Standin' arrow straight
Like a rock - Chargin' from the gate
Like a rock - Carryin' the weight
Like a rock

Like a rock - The sun upon my skin
Like a rock - Hard against the wind
Like a rock - I see myself again
Like a rock

Despite becoming a jingle for Chevy trucks, that song by Bob Seger and the Silver Bullet Band back in 1986 has a way of stopping me cold and transporting me back to why I got into this gig and why I persist.

Begging your pardon again for another melodramatic spiritualization, I often identify with some other lyrics from Seger: "So you're a little bit older and a lot less bolder than you used to be."

I had to get some supports for my feet not too long ago. My arches have fallen.

So have I on too many occasions (see Secret 6 for the dirty details).

I'm no longer as pure as the 8th grader who strolled across Princeton Theological Seminary's campus with The Rev. Harold F. Mante and said, "I just realized God wants me to come here someday to follow in your steps."

Quickly, my first mentor corrected, *"His* steps!"

That, of course, has been the challenge ever since.

People who say they love Jesus don't always follow *in His steps.*

It's Secret 14: "Corporate Christians (apostate, moderate, and evangelical) have just enough of Jesus to feel comfortable about themselves (i.e., spiritually anesthetized) but not enough to be any real good for God's sake; knowing true discipleship puts personal and vocational securities at risk."

Feeling too comfortable about yourself and too preoccupied with *your* creature comforts often

215

compromise call and contradict Christocentric and Biblical faithfulness. When personal and vocational comforts are more important than identity with the Lord in all things at all times with all people in all places as profiled in Jesus and prescribed in the Bible, *authentic* Christianity becomes corporate; which is a synonym for words like *corrupt, worldly, egocentric, base,* and *just-like-everybody-else-whose-real-Lord-is-not-Jesus.*

Here are a few examples:

- I had a business manager in Kansas City who was so proud of how she kept the church so clean; but she lost sight of the reason for the church's being. Pointing to the immaculately buffed tile floor in the narthex, she lamented, "It's too bad it will be all scuffed up after Sunday."

- There was a woman's group in that same church which decided to put new pew cushions only across the front pews on both sides of the center aisle. These were very special pew cushions–needlepointed symbols of the disciples. After months of careful and expensive craftsmanship, they were complete and installed. Then we dedicated them. While I had never seen such beautiful pew cushions, it seemed so contrary to our faith when someone brought a motion to a joint meeting of our church boards to rope them off so no one could sit on them lest they get soiled and worn. Considering most mainliners don't sit up front anyway, the motion passed easily; and caused me to wonder if we were building a museum, mausoleum, or mission.

- While mainline churches don't seem to have a problem with dissipating Christology and affronts to Biblical sexuality and the sanctity of all human life, they get really upset if you baptize somebody who was baptized as an infant. They get so caught up in their sense of "covenantal" corporate theology that they overlook the simplicity, innocence, and fidelity of the request. Somebody wants to be identified with the Lord and mark off herself or himself for Jesus. Corporates get so mad when asked, "Do you think Jesus would baptize somebody again who was baptized as a baby if they said it meant nothing to them and they want to be baptized because they love Him so much and want the whole world to know it?" Corporates have a hard time with those WWJD (What would Jesus do?) questions.

Corporate Christianity brings a tired joke to mind. It's about the disgruntled clergyman who insisted mainline Protestants will enter heaven before anyone else. When asked for proof, he declared, "It says so right in the Bible: 'The dead in Christ will rise first.' "

Here are some typical corporate questions and faithful answers:

"What if we run out of bulletins?" *Good!*
"What if we run out of parking spaces?" *Good!*
"What if there aren't enough seats?" *Good!*
"What if people show up without reservations?" *Good!*
"What if parents just drop off their children?" *Well, at least the children will be saved!*
"What if children run through the church and break things?" *I believe Jesus would rather have children running through the church and breaking things than a neat and empty building!*
"What if the sanctuary is too cold?" *Wear a sweater!*
"What if the sanctuary is too hot?" *Take off the sweater!*
"What if the church needs more money for mission?" *Excellent!*
"What will people think if we _____ (fill in the blank)?" *Who cares what people think? If you do, review Secret 1!*

Here are some favorite corporate quotes:

"We've never done it that way before."
"We're not ready to do that yet."
"We're doing just fine without that."
"We tried that once before."
"It costs too much."
"We can't afford it."

"That's not our responsibility."
"It won't work."
"It never works, but this is how we've always done it."

Here are some faithful quotes:
"Rejoice always!"
"Pray without ceasing!"
"Give thanks in all things!"
"Hold fast to what is good!"
"Release the Spirit!"
"Go for it!"
"Let's not be practical. *Let's be faithful!*"

Personally, I'm convinced corporate Christians concentrate on everything but Jesus in order to avoid their lack of fidelity to Jesus and their affronts to Christocentric, Biblical, historical, constitutional, confessional, and traditional faith as so documentable by their increasing apostasies.

Specifically, the practical behaviors of mainliners expose their beliefs are hardly distinguishable from unitarian universalists when it comes to the place of Jesus in God's plan of salvation and almost every moral issue.

Putting it another way, any connection between mainliners and Biblical Christianity is increasingly coincidental.

Jesus identified the problem in today's mainline denominations which are long on style (corporate) and short on substance (Jesus and Bible): "Beware of false prophets, who come to you in sheep's clothing but inwardly are ravenous wolves" (Matthew 7:15).

Or as Bob Dylan sang, "But the enemy I see wears a cloak of decency."

Corporate but not necessarily Christian.

Form without content.

Clearly, but painfully, another word from our enfleshed Lord exposes the fraud: "You are like whitewashed tombs, which outwardly appear beautiful, but within are full of dead people's bones and all uncleanness" (Matthew 23:27).

Jude's letter sounded the alarm about apostasy in the church – the diluting or outright rejection of Biblical ethics and the saving Lordship of Jesus (3-4):

> **Beloved, although I was very eager to write to you about our common salvation, I found it necessary to write appealing to you to contend for the faith that was once for all delivered to the saints. For certain people have crept in unnoticed who long ago were designated for this condemnation, ungodly people, who pervert the grace of our God into sensuality and deny our only Master and Lord, Jesus Christ.**

Corporately corrupt Christianity has always been a challenge to the integrity of the church.

When Christianity becomes corporate, its corruption is hardly distinguishable from the world's corruption.

The quickest way to identify corporate Christians *as well as non-Christians* is to ask one precise question: "Who is Jesus?"

If the answer does not include testimony to His unique saving Lordship and unity with Father and Holy Spirit as Son or *same substance as triune God (una substantia et tres personae)*, the person is not authentic to Christianity as exemplified in Jesus and explained in the Bible.

John wrote (1 John 4:2-3),

> By this you know the Spirit of God: every spirit that confesses that Jesus Christ has come in the flesh is from

God, and every spirit that does not confess Jesus is not from God. This is the spirit of the antichrist, which you heard was coming and now is in the world already.

Jude's solution to this problem is *authentic* Christianity: "But You, beloved, build yourselves up in your most holy faith; pray in the Holy Spirit; keep yourselves in the love of God, waiting for the mercy of our Lord Jesus Christ that leads to eternal life" (20-21).

Authentic Christians look up, stand up, and speak up for Jesus without reference to who, where, what, or when.

Authentic Christians follow Jesus and commit themselves to *be the church* without reference to who, where, what, or when.

Authentic Christians build Him up by building themselves up through worship, prayer, Bible study, fasting, sacrament, silence, stewardship, and fellowship with believers.

Authentic Christians "seek the things that are above, where Christ is" (Colossians 3:1).

It's like a nun told me many years ago, 'When tempted from God, *turn to the right.*"

In "Re-Forming Tradition: Presbyterians and Mainstream Protestantism" (*The Princeton Seminary Bulletin,* Vol. XIV, Number 1, New Series 1993), Edward A. Dowey addressed *turning to righteousness*:

The much-quoted and often-misconstrued motto, *ecclesia reformata,* s*emper reformanda,* "the church reformed must always be reformed," is part of a phrase that continues *secundum verbum Dei*, "according to the Word of God." Reform, thus, especially as a proper name, for example in Reformed tradition, means not change or alteration as such, nor does it signify a revolution that tries to start over without looking back...Our question now should not be "Are we

successful?" but "Are we faithful?" Only when Reform
roots in the Word, will we hear again another of our great
Reformed imperatives: *Sursum corda!* "Lift up your
hearts!"

The late Frank Harrington, Senior Pastor for many
years of Atlanta, Georgia's Peachtree Presbyterian Church,
expressed *authentic* Christianity juxtaposed to its
corporate counterfeit so well: "Christian education is
based, not on the reality that Jesus of Nazareth is *a* truth,
but that He is THE truth!"

Dan Qualls, Executive Pastor of Rockford, Illinois'
First Assembly Church, shared Portia Nelson's "An
Autobiography in Five Short Chapters" with me. It calls
corporates to the righteousness of God:

> Chapter 1 - I walked down the street. There is a deep
> hole in the sidewalk. I fall in. I am lost. I am helpless.
> It isn't my fault and it takes me forever to find my way
> out.

> Chapter 2 - I walk down the same street. There is a
> deep hole in the sidewalk. I pretend I don't see it. I fall
> in again. I can't believe I am in the same place. But if
> it isn't my fault, it still takes a long time to get out.

> Chapter 3- I walk down the same street. There is a
> deep hole in the sidewalk. I see it is there. I still fall in.
> It's a habit. My eyes are open. I know where I am. It
> is my fault and I get out immediately.

> Chapter 4 - I walk down the same street. There is a
> deep hole in the sidewalk. I walk around it.

> Chapter 5 - I walked down another street.

Lloyd Ogilvie, recently retired Chaplain of the United
States Senate, was introduced by someone who understands
the difference between authentic and corporate
Christianity:

221

This morning it is my profound pleasure to introduce to you an outstanding man of great eloquence and moral excellence. His ministry is unparalleled. He can walk on water, and perform great wonders. His work has changed the world. He is a homiletical dynamo, the prince of pulpiteers, a sensational man of God whose spellbinding words will capture your attention instantly. His name is Jesus Christ, and here to introduce Him is Lloyd Ogilvie.

Gary Beets, who I met many years ago as Missouri State Director of the Fellowship of Christian Athletes, gave his calling card to me which put Him into proper perspective: "If we meet and you forget me, you have lost nothing. But if you meet Jesus Christ and forget Him, you have lost everything."

Corporate Christianity is all about what's most popular in time and space.

Authentic Christianity is all about Jesus who is before and after time and space.

It's like Michael W. Smith sings so well, "It's all about You, Jesus!"

I became a pastor because of Jesus.

I remain a pastor because of Jesus.

We came to be because of Jesus.

We will always be because of Jesus.

That's why we ally ourselves with Him here and now and forever.

That's not very corporate.

But it's authentic *and saving*.

SECRET 15

Jesus is counting on you!

As a little boy on Chestnut Street in Nanticoke, Pennsylvania and Grove Street in New York City, my eyes were glued to the tube whenever it was time for Betty Boop, Popeye, Spanky, Alfalfa, Buckwheat, Howdy Doody, Soupy Sales, The Three Stooges, or Captain Kangaroo.

Though I'm not sure where the Teletubbies fit into the evolution of children's programming, my children have been equally captivated by Big Bird, Bert, Ernie, Cookie Monster, Kermit, Miss Piggie, Rolf, and so many of Jim Henson's creations.

I like Barney. I feel so good when he sings, "I love you. You love me. We're a happy family..."

My favorite children's show since its national debut on 19 February 1968 has been *Mister Rogers' Neighborhood.* I have been so thankful for the positively Christian values that Mister Rogers always impressed upon my sons as soon as he started singing at the start of every show, "It's a beautiful day in the neighborhood...Won't you be my neighbor?"

The Rev. Fred McFeely Rogers graduated from Pittsburgh Theological Seminary in 1963. He was an ordained Presbyterian pastor; and occasionally attended meetings of Pittsburgh Presbytery when I was there in the mid 90s.

I'll never forget standing with Fred and Rus Howard in the narthex of a church prior to a presbytery meeting. Rus and I thanked him for being such a positive Christian influence in our children's lives. He said, "I want you to go home and give your children a big hug from me...and you."

Though terribly saddened to lose such *a beautiful friend in the neighborhood* when Fred went home to Jesus on 27 February 2003, I rejoice in PBS' decision to continue broadcasting episodes *of Mister Rogers' Neighborhood* and I look forward to hearing him sing for generations to come:

> *It's you I like,*
> *It's not the things you wear.*
>
> *It's not the way you do your hair,*
> *But it's you I like.*
>
> *The way you are right now.*
> *The way down deep inside you.*
>
> *Not the things that hide you.*
> *Not your degrees,*
> *They're just beside you.*
>
> *But it's you I like,*
> *Every part of you.*
>
> *Your skin, your eyes, your feelings,*
> *Whether old or new.*
>
> *I hope that you'll remember*
> *Even when you're feeling blue,*
> *That it's you I like,*
> *It's you yourself, it's you,*
> *It's you I like!*

Mister Rogers - *He was always too real and authentically Christian to call The Rev. Fred McFeely Rogers!* - was Pittsburgh Theological Seminary's commencement speaker on 24 May 1994.

Considering how many people will always thank God for his positively Christian influence on their lives, I was humbled by his humility in beginning his commencement address with a tribute to his mentors and heroes:

> Thanks to reading Dr. Walther's splendid new history of our seminary, I was able to reflect on the professors who gave me the beginning of my theological education - 20 of them! Before I begin this commencement address, I'd like to read their names... [He read every name!]...I'm *very* grateful for all of them. And for all of you who carry on the best of their tradition.

Later in the address, he talked about honoring our heroes:

> My hunch is that everyone who has ever graduated from a college or a university or a seminary, anyone who has ever been able to sustain a good work, has had at least one person – and often many – who have believed in him or her. We just don't get to be competent human beings without a lot of different investments from others–often quite invisible to the eye. I'd like to give you an invisible gift: a gift of a silent minute to think about anyone who has helped you to become who you are today – any people you know who have been an important part of your journey. Some of them may be here right now.
> Some might be far away. Some may even be in heaven. But wherever they are – if they've loved you and encouraged you, and wanted what was best in life for you, they're right inside yourself, and I just feel that you deserve time on this very special occasion to devote some thought to them. So let's take a minute – a minute of silence – and think about the people who have loved us all along the way, the people who have helped us become who we are. One minute. I'll watch the clock...

225

After that silent tribute, he continued,

> Whomever you've been thinking about: Just imagine how proud they must be of you that you thought enough of them to give them credit for some of whom you've become. You know it's not the honors and the prizes and the fancy outsides of life which ultimately nourish our souls. It's the knowing that we can be trusted, that we never have to fear the truth, that ultimately there is someone who loves our very being. That's what our advocate would have us know. Maybe that's why we're the part of creation God has identified with the most!

He concluded with this prayer: "Immortal, invisible God, help us to know Your will and to do it in all the neighborhoods of Your world, through Jesus the Christ our Lord. Amen."

God knows we need more heroes like Mister Rogers – positively Christian influences for all of God's children of all ages.

Bonnie Tyler's song for the movie version of *Footloose* expressed our yearning:

> I need a hero.
> I'm holding out for a hero 'til the end of the night.
> He's gotta be strong.
> He's gotta be fast.
> And he's gotta be fresh from the fight–
>
> I need a hero.
> I'm holding out for a hero 'til morning light.
> He's gotta be sure.
> And it's gotta be soon.
> And he's gotta be larger than life...
>
> It's gonna take a superman to sweep me off my feet.
> I need a hero.

Naturally, all of our heroes end up being a little less than divine – clay feet and all the rest.

We build 'em up and watch 'em fall.

Ralph Waldo Emerson observed, "Every hero becomes at last a bore."

God cautioned through the psalmist, "Put not your trust in princes...in whom there is no salvation...Blessed is he whose help is the God of Jacob, whose hope is in the Lord his God" (see Psalm 146).

Ann Rodgers, a friend and leading religion writer for the *Pittsburgh Post-Gazette,* sent this poetic and penetrating assessment of human frailties: "You know the world's gone mad when the best rapper is a white man, the best golfer is a black man, the tallest guy in the NBA is Chinese, the Swiss hold the America's Cup, France is accusing the USA of arrogance, and the Germans don't want to go to war!"

Fortunately, our desire for a hero *or mentor who never falls or fails* can always be satisfied in Jesus.

Jesus is *so divine:* "In the beginning was the Word, and the Word was with God, and the Word was God...And the Word became flesh and dwelt among us" (see John 1:1-18).

His birth and infancy were a mighty and magical mystery tour.

His life and teachings changed history.

He beat death.

And He continues to reveal His power and change lives and resurrect anyone who invites Him into the heart as personal Lord and Savior.

Jesus is the hero who never falls or fails: "Jesus Christ is the same yesterday and today and forever" (Hebrews

13:8).

Please be assured that I am not suggesting there aren't people who have been great role models and mentors.

There's always a Mister Rogers in the neighborhood.

I've got a list.

You've got a list.

Yet it's important to recognize all of our heroes are only *human*–except for Jesus. He's *so divine.*

A really corny joke comes to mind.

Did you hear about the mystic who refused the dentist's pain killers during a root canal?

He wanted to *transcend dental medication.*

Whoa!

In a terrible analogy, Jesus transcends our human heroes to perfection here and now and forever as Emmanuel and eternal God with Father and Holy Spirit.

Rabbis have so many great stories about God's goodness and heroic character. Here's one of my favorites:

> When God was about to create the first man, He asked the opinion of angels assembled about His throne.
>
> "Create him not," said the angel of justice, "for if You do, he will commit all kinds of wickedness against others. He will be hard and cruel and dishonest and unrighteous."
>
> "Create him not," said the angel of truth, "for if You do, he will be false and deceitful to others and even to You."
>
> "Create him not," said the angel of holiness, "for if You do, he will follow what is impure in Your sight and dishonor You to Your face."
>
> Then the angel of mercy said, "Create him, Father, for when he sins and turns from the path of right, truth, and holiness, I will take him tenderly by the hand, speak loving words to him, and lead him back to You."

Sounds like our perfect hero Jesus to me!

It's like Attorney General John Ashcroft said to Cal Thomas at the beginning of America's war with Iraq, "Islam is a religion in which God requires you to send your son to die for Him...Christianity is a faith in which God sent His Son to die for you!"

An integral part of discipleship is to recall *and enflesh* our divine hero's call to be heroic: "If anyone would come after me, let him deny himself and take up his cross and follow me...Greater love has no one than this, that someone lays down his life for his friends. You are my friends if you do what I command you" (Matthew 16:24; John 15:13-14)

Succinctly, Jesus summarized our call to be heroic at the commencement of His public ministry: "Follow me, and I will make you fishers of men" (Mark 1:17).

Specifically, He instructed (Matthew 28:16-20; Acts 1:8),

Go therefore and make disciples of all nations, baptizing them in the name of the Father and of the Son and of The Holy Spirit, teaching them to observe all that I have commanded you. And behold, I am with you always, to the end of the age...You will receive power when the Holy Spirit has come upon you, and you will be my witnesses in Jerusalem and in all Judea and Samaria, and to the end of the earth.

Essentially, He said, "I am counting on you to advance the Kingdom of God *on earth as it is in heaven.*"

John Calvin commented on these texts: "Apostleship is not an empty title, but a laborious office...go to a distance, in order to spread the doctrine of salvation in every part of the world."

It's Secret 15: "Jesus is counting on you!"

Armed with His power ("You will receive power when the Holy Spirit has come upon you") and His presence ("I am with you always, to the end of the age"), we are charged to change the world for Him by pointing people to Him as saving Lord ("You will be my witnesses") and enabling everyone's saving knowledge of Him ("Go...and make disciples of all nations, baptizing them...and... teaching them to observe all that I have commanded you").

In short, Jesus is looking for heroes.

It's as if He has walked out to the mound in these late innings, tossed the ball to us, and said, "Here, pitch!"

Anything less than our best will not be acceptable.

You may recall when Jimmy Carter ran for President against Gerald Ford. His slogan was "Why Not the Best?"

It came from a meeting many years earlier with Admiral Rickover when the young Ensign Carter was being interviewed for admission to our Navy's nuclear submarine program. When Admiral Rickover asked if he had always done his best in school, Carter answered, "No." The old salt asked, "Why not?"

Why not the best?

I'm reminded of my dad listening to rationalizations about *doing my best* when falling short of expectations. He'd always say, "Just think if you woke up from an operation and the doctor said, 'Well, I did my best.' You'd think, 'But did you do it right?' "

It has become fashionable in too many parts of church and society to settle for less than our best.

"That'll do" has become the mantra of mediocrity for too many.

A young pianist leaves the instrument after only a few minutes of practice and says, "That'll do."

A young athlete ends practice prematurely and says, "That'll do."

A student gets barely passing grades and says, "That'll do."

An employee arrives late, leaves early, and says, "That'll do."

Marriages crumble under the weight of unmet needs as wives and husbands give each other that *that'll do* look.

A church looks at its mission budget and says, 'That'll do."

Here are some interesting statistics and stories about that *that'll do* attitude.

If 99% were considered *good enough,* 2,000,000 documents would be lost by the IRS in April, 12 babies would be given to the wrong parents every day, and 20,000 incorrect drug prescriptions would be written every day.

Can you imagine America and her allies having that *that'll do* attitude about Hitler and Hussein?

Do you think Fred Astaire sat down and quit when a testing director for MGM concluded, "Can't act! Slightly bald! Can dance a little!"

Do you think Beethoven, Caruso, Edison, Einstein, Newton, Tolstoy, and Churchill paid any attention to the teachers who questioned their intellect and creativity?

How do you think Vince Lombardi reacted to this evaluation: "He possesses minimal football knowledge. Lacks motivation!"?

Can you imagine Martin Luther King, Jr. saying he'd settle for anything less than equal rights for all people?

Do you think Mother Teresa ever felt O.K. about not winning the battle against poverty?

Can you imagine Jesus singing, "Give of your *less than best* to the Master"?

Have any of your heroes ever stopped before finishing the job and said, "That'll do"?

That's because *that'll do* won't do in most cases.

It's a good thing our Lord did not stop a step from the cross and say, "That'll do."

He didn't stop until the job was *finished* (see John 19:30). He gave His best – *His life* – to get the job done.

He's our hero!

And He has called us to be heroic – to be His champions!

Champions for Christ don't say, "I think I can." They say, "I know I can!" James believed in the power of positive thinking: "He must believe and not doubt, because he who doubts is like a wave of the sea, blown and tossed by the wind" (1:6).

Champions for Christ don't say, "I'm too young...I'm too poor... I'm too old...I'm not able." They say with Elihu, "It is the spirit in a man" (see Job 32).

Champions for Christ don't say, "Everybody has their limits." They say, "I can do all things through Him who gives me strength" (Philippians 4:13).

Champions for Christ don't say, "It's impossible." They say, "Nothing is impossible with God" (Luke 1:37).

Champions for Christ don't say, "The odds aren't in my favor." They say, "They have not gained the victory over me" (see Psalm 129).

That'll do won't do for heroes.

Burly and Donna Chapman, owners of Dogwood Hills Golf Course in Claysville, Pennsylvania, are champions for Christ. They know Jesus is counting on them.

They are so committed to Jesus that they close their golf course every Easter Day. They don't think it's right to golf on the morning set aside to honor God for resurrection realities certified in Jesus. And if you know anything about the business side of the game, you know Sundays *and especially holidays that fall on Sundays* generate most of the annual income.

When I asked them why they shut down the course every Easter Day and lose *all of that money,* Donna said without hesitation, "Because we feel it honors the Lord."

That's heroic.

Being a hero for Jesus is sacrificing self-absorption and selfishness for selfless service to honor God.

Let me put it another way.

Turn to Acts 29.

You say there is no Acts 29.

Not true.

It's being written right now by you and me.

It's Secret 15.

ABOUT THE AUTHOR
vita

▶ Born on 2 March 1952 in Washington, D.C.

▶ Graduate of King's College (A.B., *maxima cum laude,* 1974), Princeton Theological Seminary (Master of Divinity, 1977), and Drew University (Doctor of Ministry, 1982).

▶ Attended the Ecumenical Study Program in Heidelberg, Germany (1974) which included studies in Old Testament, New Testament, and Christian-Marxist dialogue along with study tours to the World Council of Churches in Geneva and Gregorian in Rome.

▶ Made six independent study tours to Israel and Sinai beginning in 1982.

▶ Served as an adjunct professor of expository preaching at Nazarene Theological Seminary beginning in 1982.

▶ Articles published in several newspapers and journals. Sermons published in several periodicals including Preaching, Pulpit Digest, and Vital Sermons of the Day. Praying Like Jesus, an exposition of the Lord's Prayer, was published by Pedestal Press in 1986. Featured in Great Preaching - 1992, 1993, 1994 (The Preaching Library) and Abingdon Preaching Annual (1995-1999). Golf in the Real Kingdom (2000), Don't Forget This! (2000), and God's Top Ten List (2001) were published by CSS Publishing Company.

▶ Served as Chairman of Pittsburgh Presbytery's Evangelism and Congregational Development Unit, Member of General Council and Executive Presbyter Search Committee, President of Valley High School Wrestling Boosters, President of New Kensington-Arnold Clergy Association, and appointed to Youth Commission by Westmoreland County Juvenile Court. Served on Washington Presbytery's Committee on Ministry, Preparation for Ministry, and represented presbytery as reader of denominational ordination examinations. Serves on Blackhawk Presbytery's General Council, Preparation for Ministry, and chairs the Worship Committee.

▶ Served as pastor of churches in Pennsylvania, New Jersey, Ohio, North Carolina, and Missouri ranging in size from 100 to 2600.

- Tony Campolo has said, "Good sermons are hard to come by. But Bob Kopp comes by them with uncanny regularity."

- Eagle Scout without palms, Order of the Arrow (Brotherhood), B-tennis player, and 8-12 handicap golfer (addicted).

- Began his ministry at Bethany on 1 August 2001 with wife Leslie and sons Ben, David, James, Daniel, and Matthew.

Bethany Presbyterian Church exists to honor God and share the unconditional love of Jesus with everyone.

God's Top Ten List
A Prescription For
Positive Living
by
Robert R. Kopp

God's Top Ten List approaches the Ten Commandments not as a list of do's and don'ts but as a path toward personal peace and social renewal. In messages liberally sprinkled with gripping illustrations, Kopp explores the timeless truth of the commandments, and notes that they are God's recipe for achieving a happy and satisfying life.

Robert R. Kopp is pastor of Center Presbyterian Church in McMurray, Pennsylvania. A *maxima cum laude* graduate of King's College in Wilkes-Barre, Pennsylvania, he has also earned degrees from Princeton Theological Seminary (M.Div.) and Drew University (D.Min.). In addition to having served as adjunct professor of expository preaching at Nazarene Theological Seminary, he has pastored churches in Pennsylvania, New Jersey, Ohio, North Carolina, and Missouri. Kopp's sermons have been featured in such periodicals as *Preaching*, *Pulpit Digest*, and *Vital Sermons of the Day*, as well as in *Great Preaching* and the *Abingdon Preaching Annual*. Kopp is the author of *Don't Forget This!* and *Golf In The Real Kingdom* (CSS).

ISBN 0-7880-1786-1   Price $8.95

Also available in these formats

MT 17861   Disk $8.95
MW 17861   Sermon Prep $8.95
CSS Publishing Co.   Lima, Ohio 45802
Phone 1-800-537-1030   Fax 1-419-228-9184
E-mail orders@csspub.com

Good sermons are hard to come by — but Bob Kopp comes by them with uncanny regularity. Kopp understands our culture as few preachers do, and addresses crucial issues of our time with biblical faithfulness and prophetic insight.

Tony Campolo noted author and preacher
Professor of Sociology, Eastern College

Robert Kopp's writing is original, intriguing, provocative, biblical, and at times confrontational. One thing he never is: boring!

Michael Duduit, Editor *Preaching* magazine

God's Top Ten List

List

A Prescription For Positive Living

ISBN 0-7880-1786-1   Price: $8.95

MT 17861   disk: $8.95

MW 17861   sp: $8.95

Publisher: CSS Publishing Company   Lima, Ohio 45802

Phone: 1-800-537-1030   Fax: 1-419-228-9184

E-mail: orders@csspub.com

Visit our website: www.csspub.com

Impact Christian Books

332 Leffingwell Ave., Suite 101
Kirkwood, MO 63122

AVAILABLE AT YOUR LOCAL BOOKSTORE, OR YOU MAY
ORDER DIRECTLY. Toll-Free, order-line only M/C, DISC,
or VISA 1-800-451-2708.

Visit our Website at *www. impactchristianbooks.com*

Write for *FREE* Catalog.